LANCASTER
IN
50
BUILDINGS

BILLY F. K. HOWORTH

AMBERLEY

Lancaster in 50 Buildings ist Manfred und Christel Knorr, für ihre Liebe und Unterstützung im Verlauf der Jahre gewidmet.

First published 2018

Amberley Publishing, The Hill, Stroud
Gloucestershire GL5 4EP

www.amberley-books.com

British Library Cataloguing in Publication Data.
A catalogue record for this book is available from the British Library.

ISBN 978 1 4456 7662 3 (print)
ISBN 978 1 4456 7663 0 (ebook)

Origination by Amberley Publishing.
Printed in Great Britain.

Contents

Introduction

The history of the city of Lancaster is not only a story of great buildings and architecture, but also a record of the great events and businesses that shaped them.

Since the earliest days of the Roman occupation, Lancaster has played a key part in many events that influenced not only local history but also the nation.

From the infamous Pendle Witch Trials to the city's involvement in the North Atlantic slave trade, through to the mechanisation of industry in the nineteenth century, Lancaster has been at the forefront.

This book features many notable buildings, from town halls, railway stations and hospitals, to factories, theatres and bridges, with every part of Lancaster's history examined.

In the twentieth century, Lancaster underwent many changes and in the process many notable buildings were lost, old streets disappeared, and parts of the city's history were forgotten. The surviving buildings not only give us a glimpse into the past but also tell us their remarkable stories.

By shining a light onto some of the lesser-known and often overlooked buildings that the city is home to, I hope that this book will give you a clearer overview of how Lancaster's history has been pivotal in creating the fabric of the city that we see today.

I have illustrated the book throughout with recent photographs that showcase these notable buildings, and with a few older images to show how the sites have changed.

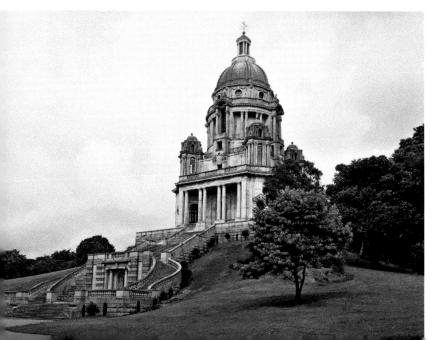

Ashton Memorial, Williamson Park.

Key

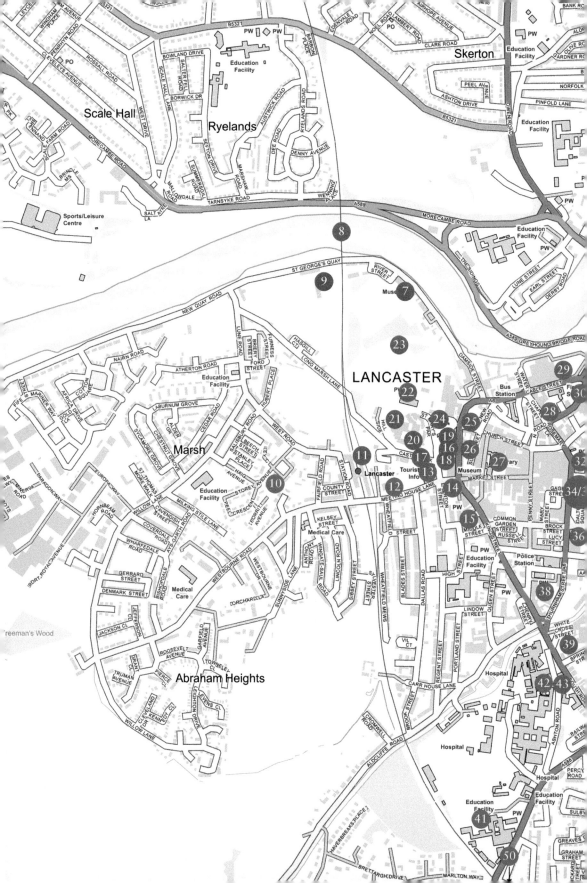

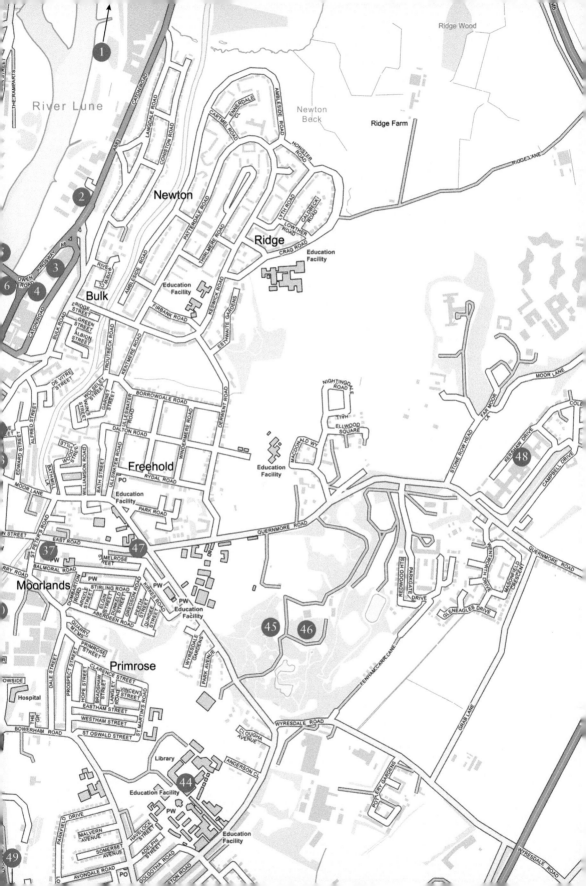

The 50 Buildings

1. Lune Aqueduct

The first stopping point on our journey into Lancaster's important buildings is the Lune Aqueduct. Although it isn't a building in the strictest sense, it is arguably one of the most important structures in the history of the city.

In 1772, the proposed route of the Lancaster Canal was surveyed by Robert Whitworth and later resurveyed by John Longbotham, Robert Dickinson and Richard Beck in 1791. A final survey was carried out in the same year by engineer John Rennie.

In 1792, the proposers of the canal sought an Act of Parliament, which created the Company of Proprietors of the Lancaster Canal Navigation. John Rennie was officially appointed as the canal's engineer in July 1792, and work began immediately on the route between Preston and Tewitfield. One year later, a second Act of Parliament was obtained that approved the construction of the Glasson Dock branch, which would allow access from the canal to the sea at Glasson.

The main obstacle around Lancaster was how to get the canal across the River Lune and it was decided that an impressive aqueduct should be constructed, allowing boats to travel across the river. John Rennie, engineer of the canal, also designed the new aqueduct and it was constructed by architect Alexander Stevens.

Towards the end of the construction, there was a rush to finish the aqueduct before the winter and men were ordered to work around the clock. This pushed the cost of the project over budget by around £30,000, with the final cost around £50,000. In 1797 the aqueduct was opened, and boats were able to travel from Preston to Tewitfield.

The Lancaster Canal was originally planned to run from Westhoughton in Lancashire to Kendal in Cumbria. To achieve this, the section of canal close to the River Ribble also needed an aqueduct; however, due to the lack of available funds after the overspend on the Lune Aqueduct, there was no money to construct another across the River Ribble. This meant that the Lancaster Canal was never connected to the main canal network and instead the southern parts of the canal were leased to the Leeds and Liverpool Canal.

In 1813, work began on the canal northwards from Tewitfield towards Kendal and was completed in 1819. The construction of the Glasson Dock branch began later in 1819 and it was officially opened in 1826.

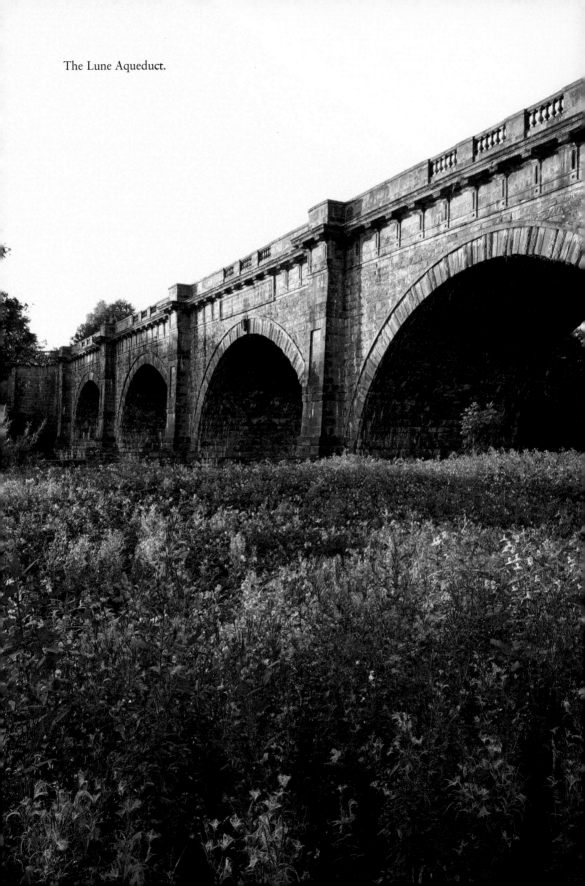

The Lune Aqueduct.

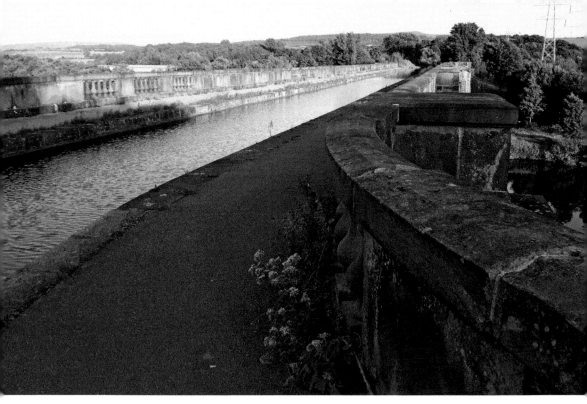

Lancaster Canal and footpath atop the Lune Aqueduct.

2. Lancaster Wagon Works

The Lancaster Railway Carriage and Wagon Company was established in 1863, overseen by prominent local Dr Edward de Vitre who served as the company's first chairman.

Two years later the business moved to its newly built site alongside the River Lune and Caton Road, which covered 15 acres. Edward Graham Paley, the prominent local architect, designed the company offices and workshops, including the notable gateway mounted with a clock. Importantly, the new location was next to the 'Little' North Western Railway that provided easy transportation for finished goods.

The company's main focus was on the construction of wagons, railway carriages and trams, as well as manufacturing wheels and axles. Interestingly, the business also provided a hire service for their wagons.

Their goods were sold both nationally and internationally and they developed a reputation for manufacturing high-quality rolling stock. These were sold far and wide, from Australia and Argentina, to India, South Africa and Brazil.

In 1902, the company was taken over and merged with several other companies to form the Metropolitan Amalgamated Railway Carriage and Wagon Company, which was based mainly around Manchester and Birmingham. Lancaster Wagon Works fell into a rapid decline as many new orders were diverted to other sites within the new company.

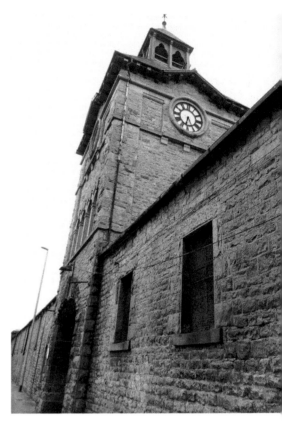

Right: The gatehouse and clock.

Below: Exterior of the old Lancaster Wagon Works building.

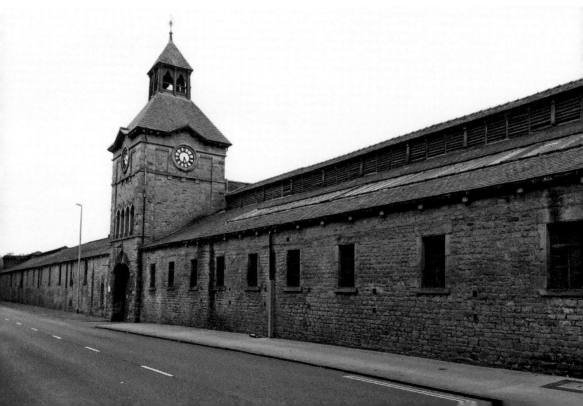

In 1902, they worked alongside another local company, Gillows, to create a carriage for the new royal train of King Edward VII. A year later they were also awarded the contract to build electric trams for the Lancaster Corporation. These were the last major contracts that the company completed.

The factory closed in 1908 with around 2,000 men made redundant. At its height, the company was the second largest employer in Lancaster, employing approximately 1,800 people during the 1880s. Unusually, the employees were given several perks, including a subsidised canteen, unionisation and the highest wages in the town.

Later, the factory was used for the internment of POWs during the First World War. One of its most well-known officers was Robert Graves, who wrote about his time in Lancaster in his autobiography *Goodbye to All That*. Since 1923, the site has been occupied by another local business, Standfast & Barracks.

3. Kingsway Baths

Located on the edge of the city is one of Lancaster's forgotten buildings that served the local community for almost sixty years.

The Kingsway Baths were built to replace the early Gregson Baths on Cable Street, which were in urgent need of updating.

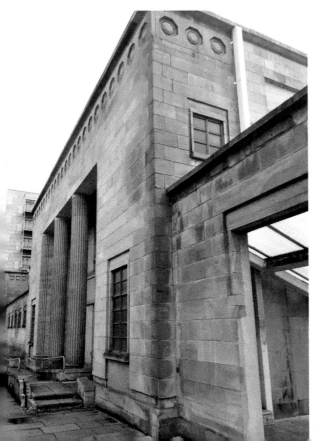

Exterior of the old Kingsway Baths.

In 1938, the Baths and Recreation Grounds Committee, chaired by the mayor of Lancaster, Henry Warbrick, was trying to find a permanent site for their new baths. It had previously been suggested that the land close to the Bridge Houses would be a suitable location as the site had rarely been used, apart from hosting fairs.

It was decided that the site would be a suitable option and construction began the same year. The new site was also designed to house the local transport depot, which was completed shortly after the baths.

In July 1939, the Kingsway Baths were officially opened by the Minister for Health, Walter E. Elliot. Unfortunately, Warbrick died in 1938 and never saw the completed baths.

Over the following decades, the building underwent many alterations to keep it up to date with the changing needs of the city's residents, including the addition of new saunas during the 1970s and a new sports hall in the mid-1980s. In 1987 it was suggested that the adjacent depot could be used to expand the centre; however, the plans were scrapped a year later.

The complex remained the town's most important recreational centre until 1997 when it officially closed, and the new Salt Ayre Sports Centre opened. Today, only the façade of the original building remains and its role in the community has been lost.

Old photograph of the original interior and swimming pool.

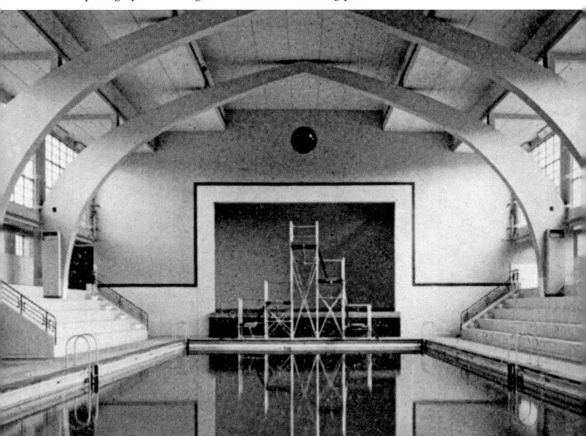

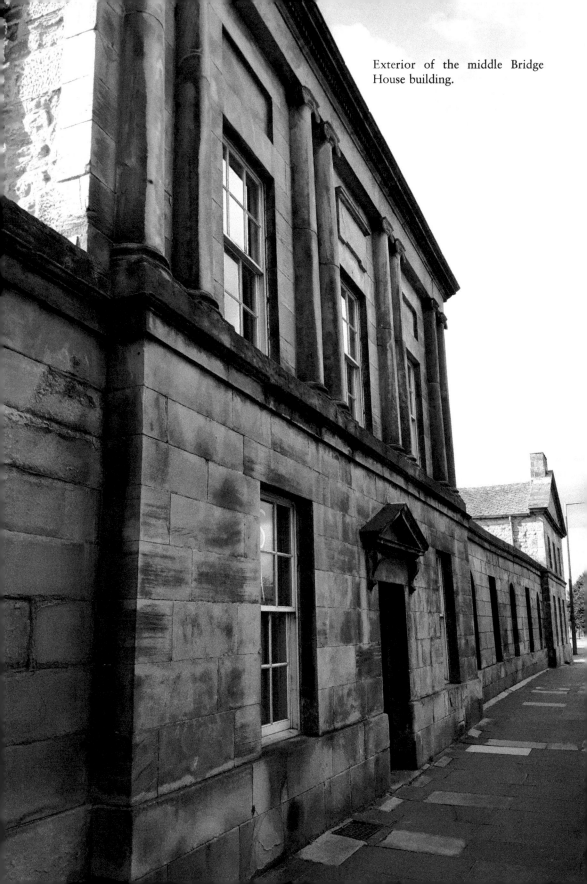

Exterior of the middle Bridge
House building.

4. Bridge Houses

Neglected and often overlooked are the Bridge Houses, close to Skerton Bridge.

The three houses were designed by Thomas Harrison and originally built as part of the development of Skerton Bridge in 1787. Unusually, the houses are not mentioned in any records or specifications from the time and do not appear on any of the original drawings.

It is believed that the houses were at least partly used for the payment of tolls for the use of the new bridge, and it is known that they were also private residences, as well as home to a public house, which possibly occupied the central building. In 1794, the first inn at this site is recorded, with the innkeeper listed as John Martin. The inn was later known as the Bridge Inn.

Later, at the beginning of the nineteenth century, the houses continued to be used as residences and as a public house, with records from the 1810s and 1820s listing the names of the innkeepers. It is not known when the Bridge Inn finally closed, but by the 1890s all three buildings had become private homes.

During the twentieth century the Bridge Houses were still used as residences but by the 1920s the area was starting to suffer due to the new roads and increased traffic on Skerton Bridge. By the 1980s, the buildings were in a poor condition and were temporarily saved in 1985 when a restaurant opened, using two of the houses. Afterwards, the buildings and surrounding area continued to decline, until the recent redevelopment of the Kingsway Baths site.

The Bridge House buildings.

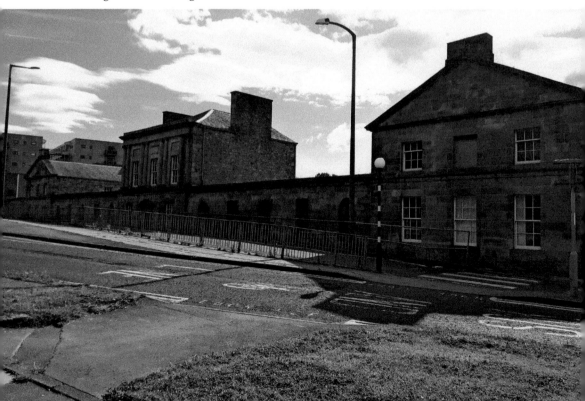

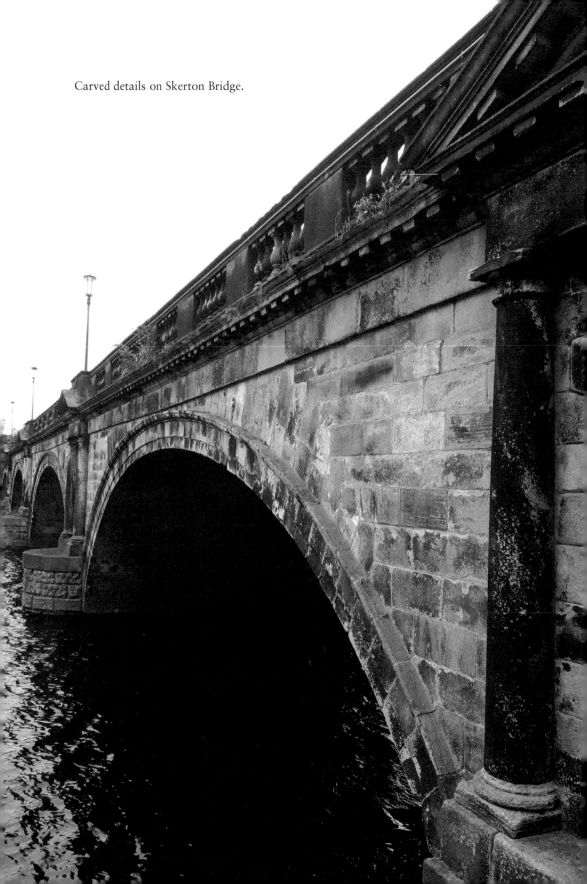

Carved details on Skerton Bridge.

5. Skerton Bridge

One of the earliest bridges in Lancaster is Skerton Bridge, designed by architect Thomas Harrison.

The bridge was designed as an entry for a competition held in 1782. The aim of the competition was to find a design for the new bridge that was to cross the River Lune, replacing the old medieval bridge, known as the Old Loyne Bridge.

Thomas Harrison's design was chosen as the winning entry and after some minor alterations the first stone was laid in 1783. It took four years to construct the new bridge, at a cost of around £14,000. It officially opened in September 1787. An interesting design feature of the bridge is that it is supported by five elliptical arches. It was also the first bridge in England to have a flat road surface.

In 1839, the bridge was repaired and repointed, with work overseen by local architect Edmund Sharpe. Later, in 1849, an additional arch was added to the southern end of the bridge to allow the 'Little' North Western Railway to pass beneath.

Originally, the bridge supported traffic travelling both ways; however, with the opening of the Greyhound Bridge Road in the 1970s the bridge became part of the one-way system. In 2018, Skerton Bridge was temporarily reinstated for two-way traffic due to the renovation of Greyhound Bridge.

The bridge is notable not only for being a key structure in Lancaster but also for the effect it had on Thomas Harrison and his career. Skerton Bridge was his first major project and lead on to later work, including Stramongate Bridge in Kendal and the redesign of Lancaster Castle.

Skerton Bridge looking southwards.

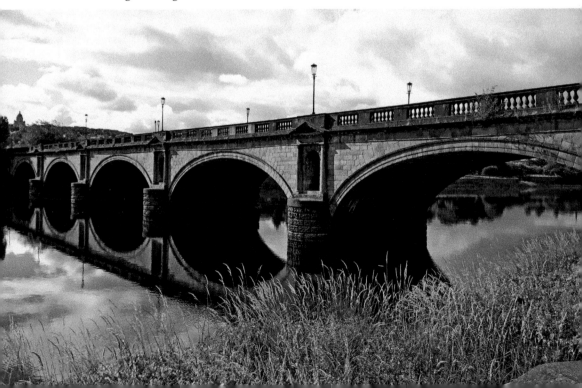

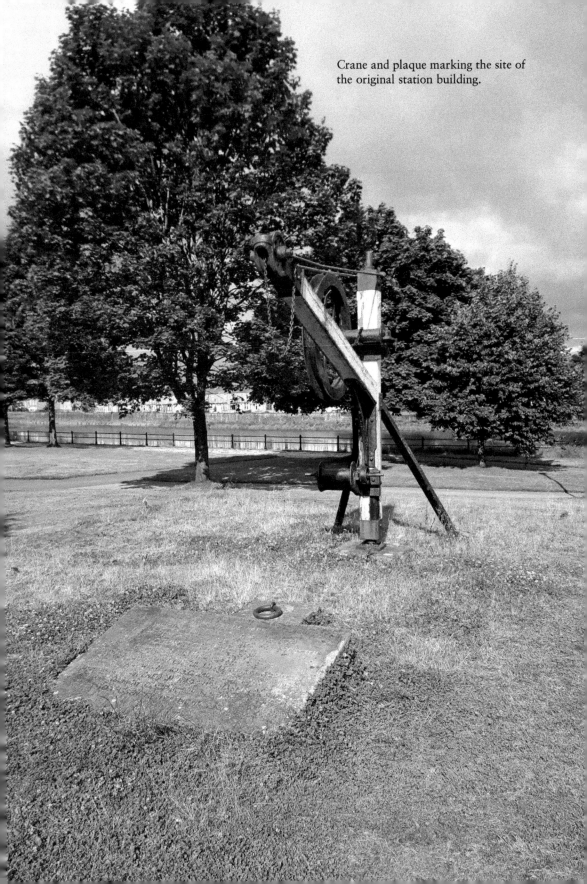

Crane and plaque marking the site of the original station building.

6. Lancaster Green Ayre Railway Station

Since the mid-nineteenth century, Lancaster has been served by the railways, some of which are no longer visible.

In 1848, the Morecambe Harbour and Railway Company constructed a railway that connected the Lancaster Green Ayre Railway Station to the Morecambe Harbour Railway Station. The station building was designed by local architect Edward Paley. At the same time, the company also constructed the first Greyhound Bridge, using wood, which carried the new railway over the River Lune.

Between 1862 and 1864, the wooden bridge was replaced with a wrought-iron bridge and the route was electrified in 1908. One of the most unusual features of

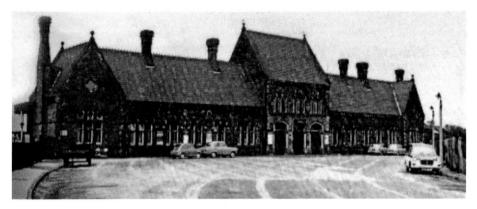

Old photograph of the original station building.

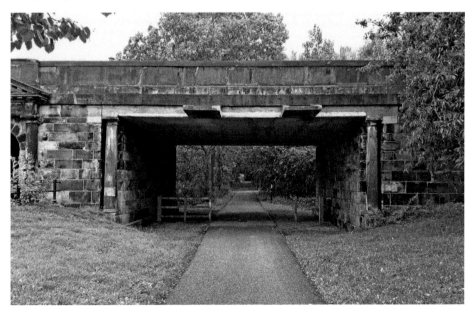

Train tunnel beneath Skerton Bridge.

the bridge is its noteworthy westward curve across the River Lune, which has been a feature of the bridge since 1864. In 1911, the second bridge was demolished, and the current bridge was constructed.

The railway, which connected Morecambe and Wennington via Green Ayre, was a victim of the Beeching Axe (a reduction of route network and restructuring of the railways in Great Briatin) and was closed in 1966 along with Greyhound Bridge, although the station building continued to be used by freight trains until 1976, when it was closed and demolished.

The old railway bridge was converted to accommodate road vehicles, reopening in 1972. The bridge underwent significant maintenance in 2018 when it was closed for most of the year for engineering work to ensure its long-term survival.

7. The Old Customs House

On St George's Quay stands one of Lancaster's most important Georgian buildings, which tells the story of Lancaster's role in the North Atlantic slave trade. The area known as St George's Quay developed at the height of the slave trade and became the commercial hub of the city throughout the late eighteenth century.

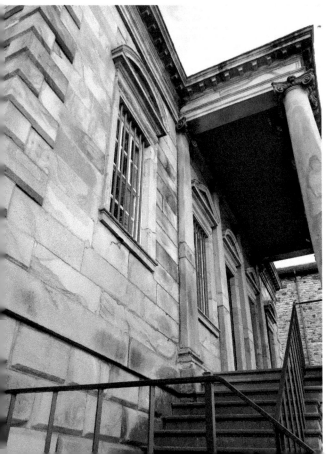

Carved details of the Old Customs House.

Between 1750 and 1755, this area along the banks of the River Lune changed from barren land to a fully functioning port, complete with quayside, mooring points, warehouses, inns, shipbuilders and, most importantly, a customs house.

The development of the Port of Lancaster came through an Act of Parliament in 1749. The aim of the Act was to improve the navigation of the Lune, whilst at the same time set about creating the Port of Lancaster and the Port Commission. The Act set out many legal requirements, from the construction of navigation markers near the Lune Estuary mouth, to the construction of warehouses, bonded warehouses and a building where legal documentation could be completed and taxes could be paid.

The warehouses were some of the first buildings constructed and can still be seen. The Customs House was built much later, in 1764. It was designed by architect Richard Gillow, the son of Robert Gillow who founded the famous Gillows of Lancaster business.

Richard designed the Customs House in a Palladian style, using elements of classic Greek and Roman architecture. It was built using local stone quarried from a site near Ellel, on the outskirts of Lancaster. From surviving records, we know that the construction took around fifteen months and cost £784, 7s and 1/2d.

Upon its completion, it became the working heart of the port, overseen by the customs officer who had an office on the first floor. The upper floor was used for the day-to-day transactions and payment of taxes, whereas the ground floor was used for weighing the goods that had been brought into the port. The warehouses next to the Customs House were constructed in 1797 as bonded warehouses, used to hold the most expensive goods being imported.

The Customs House was used until 1882 when its duties were moved to Barrow-in-Furness. Since 1985, the Customs House and adjoining warehouse have been home to the Lancaster Maritime Museum.

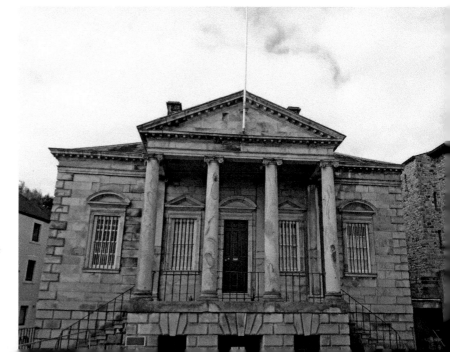

Exterior of the Old Customs House.

8. Carlisle Bridge

One of Lancaster's most important structures is Carlisle Bridge, which carries the West Coast Mainline across the River Lune northwards towards Carlisle and Scotland.

The Lancaster & Carlisle Railway was designed by Joseph Locke and John Edward Errington, with the Carlisle Bridge section being built by a syndicate of Thomas Brassey, William Mackenzie and John Stephenson.

The first bridge consisted of stone supports with spans in laminated timber, which allowed construction to progress quickly between 1844 and 1846. The bridge officially opened in 1847.

The bridge underwent alterations in 1866 when the wooden beams were replaced with iron girders, and later in 1962–63 when the iron girders were replaced with steel and concrete. The railway line was electrified in 1974.

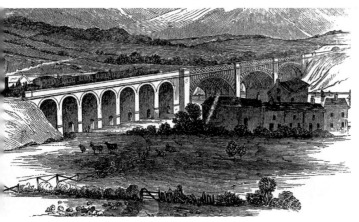

Left: Old sketch of the original Carlisle Bridge.

Below: Carlisle Bridge looking northwards.

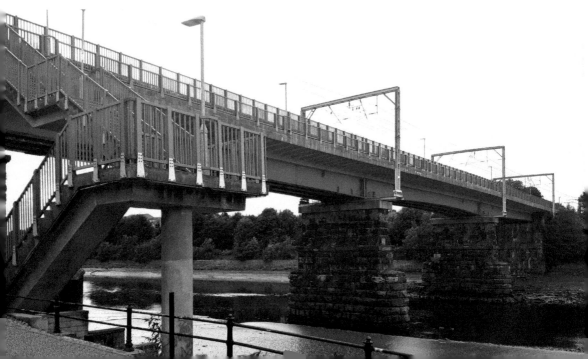

9. St George's Works and Lune Mills

Located along St George's Quay is the imposing St George's Works, part of the Lune Mills manufacturing site, which produced linoleum.

James Williamson senior established Williamson & Co., a coated fabrics business, during the 1840s, which grew to become one of the largest linoleum-producing factories in Europe.

In 1855, Williamson constructed St George's Works close to the River Lune and by the 1860s had expanded the site. Land along the quayside was cheap and the water could be used during the manufacturing process as well as providing a method of transportation.

His son James Williamson junior, who would become Lord Ashton, helped to drive the business forward and in 1871 purchased the site of the old Lune Shipbuilding Company to expand production. The new Lune Mills site covered an area of around 21 acres.

The factory building was constructed using the red bricks that were left over from the brickworks previously located on the site. The new factory was equipped with the most up-to-date equipment for producing oilcloth and linoleum, with the products aimed at the working class.

In 1875, James Williamson junior took over the business due to his father's ill health, ushering in a new period of expansion for the business and establishing

Exterior of the old St George's Works building.

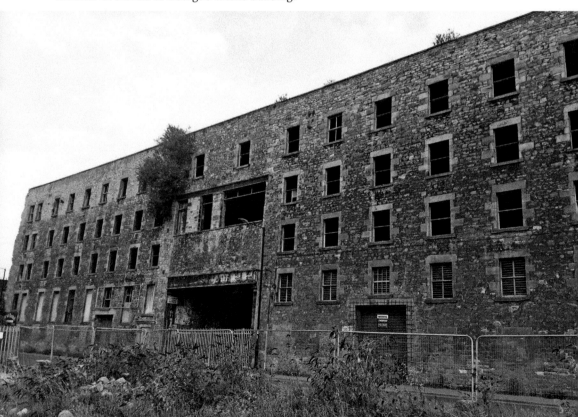

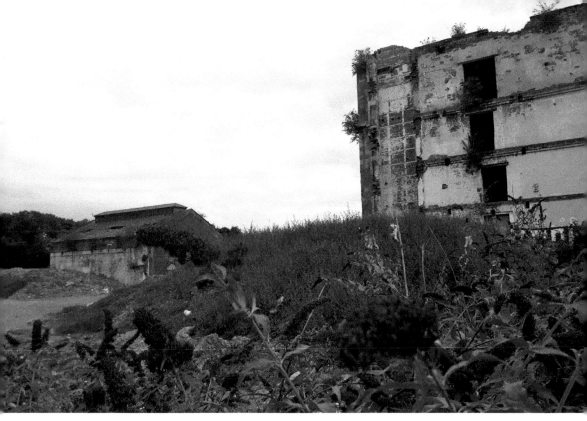

The site after demolition of some of the original buildings.

a monopoly in the process. In 1883, the Lune Mills site was connected to the Glasson branch line by a station on the site.

By 1894, Williamson's employed around 2500 men, and by 1911 employed around 25 per cent of Lancaster's working men. Upon James Williamson junior's death in 1930, over 2,000 of his workers attended the funeral and created a procession to mark the passing of this extraordinary man.

His company continued to grow, and in 1944 celebrated its centenary. But increasing competition from abroad, accompanied by the effect of two wars and the economic downturn, was beginning to cause problems for the business. By the 1950s and 1960s, the town's once major business had fallen into a poor state and subsequently merged with other companies. In 2001, the Lancaster factories closed.

Although most of the site has now been regenerated, the history of the company and the name Williamson will never be forgotten.

10. Westfield Memorial Village

One of the hidden gems of Lancaster is the Westfield Memorial Village, built to house ex-servicemen who had been injured during the First World War.

Shortly after the war ended in 1918, a committee held a meeting to discuss how the needs of retuning soldiers could be addressed. It was acknowledged that some

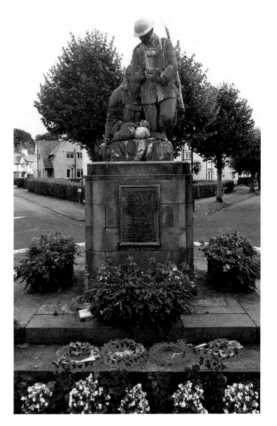

Right: The memorial at the centre of the village.

Below: Original map showing the layout of the village.

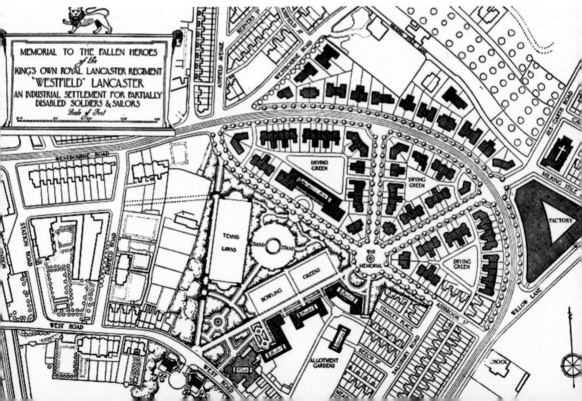

MEMORIAL TO THE FALLEN HEROES
of the
KING'S OWN ROYAL LANCASTER REGIMENT
"WESTFIELD" LANCASTER
AN INDUSTRIAL SETTLEMENT FOR PARTIALLY
DISABLED SOLDIERS & SAILORS
Scale of Feet

would be unable to earn a living without assistance, and it was decided that to aid in their rehabilitation a new housing development would be constructed to provide them with suitable accommodation.

The village was designed by local architect Thomas Mawson and supported by Herbert Lushington Storey, a member of the prominent Storey family. The family donated the Westfield Estate, which covered around 16 acres, and public donations were used to construct the village.

Construction work began in 1919 and brought together many of Lancaster's well-known philanthropists as well as the local population, many of whom had lost their own sons during the war. Priority for housing was given to those who had served as members of the King's Own Royal Regiment and the village was officially opened by Field Marshal Douglas Haig in 1924.

The village comprised a mixture of housing, from homes for married couples to hostel accommodation for unmarried residents. It was laid out in the style of a traditional village, complete with bowling green, gardens and tree-lined streets. The centrepiece of the village is the evocative memorial created by Jennifer Delahunt in 1926.

The main aim of the village was not only to provide housing, but also a source of employment for soldiers who had been injured and were unable to return to their former jobs. Westfield House served as a training centre and efforts were made to provide work, from manufacturing pipes and tailoring, to making clocks and umbrellas.

However, the government was less supportive of memorial villages and took a national approach to subsidising housing and providing training. By 1943, the village consisted of sixty-eight houses and cottages, with the village expanding further after the Second World War and during the 1990s.

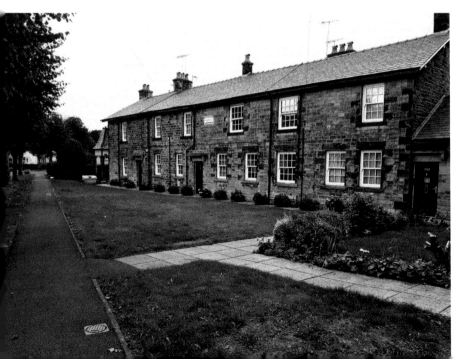

Exterior of one of the buildings on Storey Avenue.

11. Lancaster (Castle) Railway Station

Lancaster has a long and fascinating history connected to the railways that dates back to 1840. It is often forgotten that the station that now serves the city was not the first one to be built to serve it.

The first railway opened in 1840 and was known as the Lancaster and Preston Junction Railway, its station located in Greaves.

The present railway opened in 1846 as the Lancaster and Carlisle Railway. The station was known as Lancaster (Castle) Railway Station and was designed by William Tite. In 1852, the building was extended at the new tower, which includes a carving of the city's coat of arms.

In 1879, the railway became part of the London and North Western Railway, and in 1923 became part of the London, Midland & Scottish railway.

Between 1900 and 1906, the station underwent significant remodelling, with a new station building constructed on the eastern side of the station along with new platforms. The new platforms, known as 5 and 6, served the Midland Railway route to Morecambe via Lancaster Green Ayre Railway Station until 1966.

Until 1969 the station was still known as Lancaster (Castle) Station. Platform 6 was removed in 1973 and a year later the West Coast Mainline was electrified.

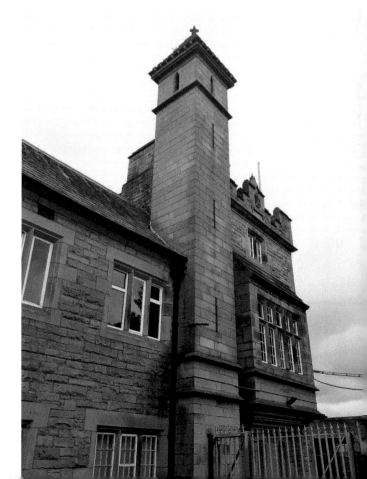

The tower building on the northbound side of the station.

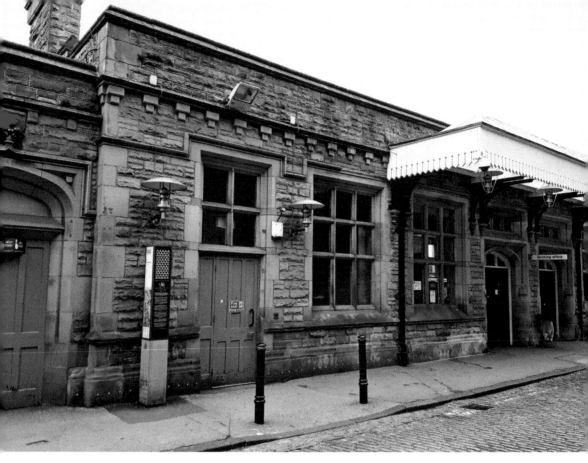

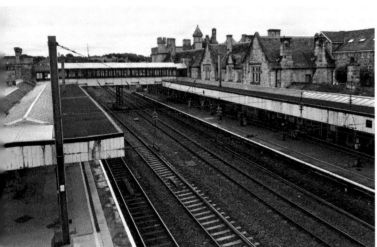

Above: Exterior of the station building on the southbound side of the station.

Left: The station buildings and tracks.

Interestingly, the railway line had many smaller branches, including a freight line that ran west from the station behind Williamson's linoleum mill on St George's Quay and onwards to Glasson Dock. Ashton Hall was also served by its own private platform, along with the right to stop the trains when necessary. Today, the station is one of the main stations on the West Coast Main Line.

12. Lancaster Friends Meeting House

Tucked away close to Lancaster Railway Station is the Religious Society of Friends' Meeting House.

The history of the Quakers in Lancaster dates to 1652 when George Fox, founder of the Quakers, visited the city. Following Fox's visit, meetings for members were held at various houses until the first Meeting House was constructed in 1677, on a road then known as Kiln Lane. However, as the religion was viewed as non-conformist, they were not granted any legal protections until the Toleration Act was passed in 1689.

The central section of the current Meeting House dates to 1708 and by 1719 the street was known as Meeting House Lane. The building was further extended on the east side in 1779, and on the west side between 1789 and 1790.

The building is built in a simple style compared to the grand architecture that is found in other religious buildings throughout the town. The grounds around the Meeting House were originally used as a burial ground.

Many of Lancaster's most famous merchants who made their wealth during the Georgian period through the North Atlantic slave trade were members of Quaker families.

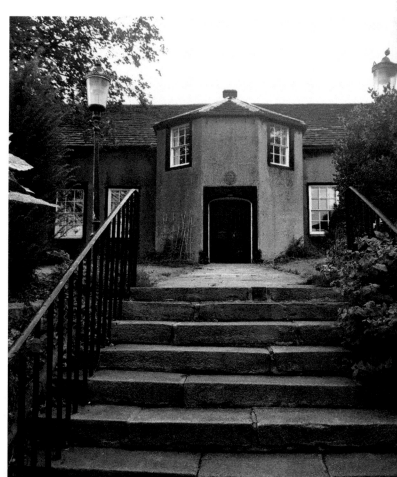

Steps and garden leading to the Friends Meeting House building.

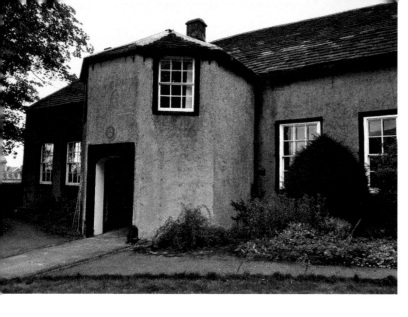

Exterior of the Friends
Meeting House
building.

The Quakers also founded the Friends' School in 1690, which they ran until 1968 when it became the independent George Fox School, until its closure in 1988. The Quaker graveyard, which was first used in 1661, can be found on Wyresdale Road, across from the entrance to Williamson Park.

13. The Storey Institute

The Storey Institute was constructed between 1887 and 1891 and was designed by leading architectural firm Paley, Austin and Paley at a cost of around £12,000.

It was funded by local industrialist Thomas Storey to replace the outdated Lancaster Mechanics' Institute. The aim of the institute was to promote science, art, literature and technical skills, as well as to commemorate the golden jubilee of Queen Victoria.

The building housed a library, reading room, laboratory, lecture room and music room, as well as a school of art, picture gallery and accommodation for the resident caretaker.

In 1891, the building was officially named The Storey Institute to honour Thomas Storey and in 1889 held its first art exhibition, which included paintings by Constable and Gainsborough. The building also houses a curved stained-glass window designed by local company Shrigley and Hunt.

The building was extended between 1906 and 1908 and designed by Austin and Paley. Herbert Lushington Storey, the son of Thomas Storey, gave £10,000 towards the new extension, which was to commemorate the accession of Edward VII.

During the twentieth century, the building was used for many different purposes, including as a public library, city art gallery and girls' grammar school, and was the home of the Lancaster College of Art until 1982.

In 1968, the art collection was moved to the Lancaster City Museum and by the 1980s the gallery was rarely used. The walled garden behind the building, now known as the Tasting Garden, was created in 1998, and today the building is home to many small businesses, exhibition areas, workshops and a café.

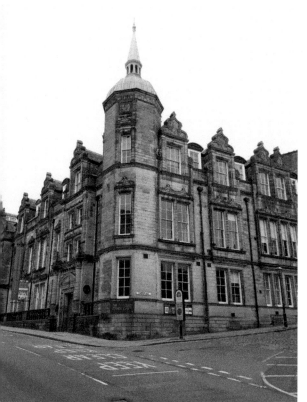

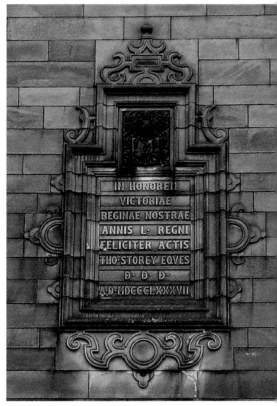

Above left: The Storey Institute from Meeting House Lane.

Above right: Carved dedication on the building's façade.

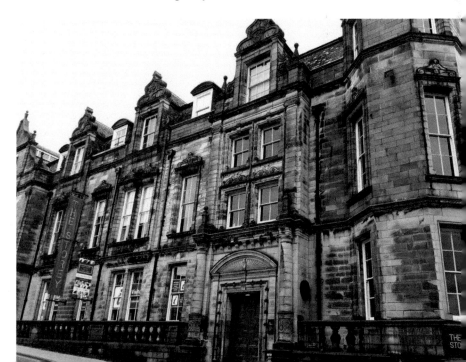

Exterior of
the Storey
Institute.

14. The Royal Kings Arms Hotel

One of the city's most prominent and famous hotels is the Royal Kings Arms.

The early history of the hotel is unknown, but it is possible that the first landlord was James Hardman, who unfortunately lost all his possessions during Lancaster's siege by the Royalists in 1643.

A year later, John Hunter was recorded as being the landlord of the hotel, and through surviving records we know that he had to pay tax on ten fireplaces. By 1689, the hotel had to pay tax on sixteen fireplaces and was owned by Randall Hunter. Interestingly, the records also note that the rooms in the hotel had usual names, including 'Halfe Moone' and 'Star Chamber'.

In 1701, the hotel was listed for sale and in 1713 the hotel may have briefly changed its name to the Queens Arms in honour of Queen Anne. By 1825, the hotel was under the control of John Pitt and had become the town's main coaching inn, with several coaches stopping daily.

Joseph Sly became the landlord during the mid-nineteenth century and entertained many important guests at the hotel. His guests included Queen Adelaide and Prince Louis Napoleon of France, as well as writers including Wilkie

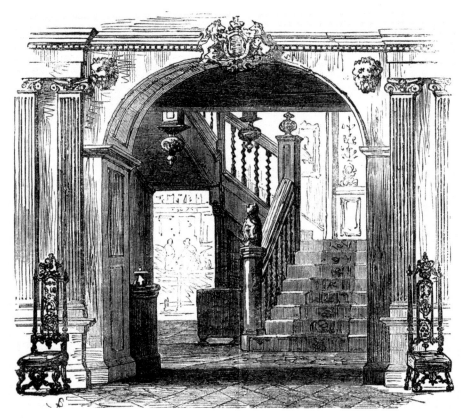

Old sketch of the interior.

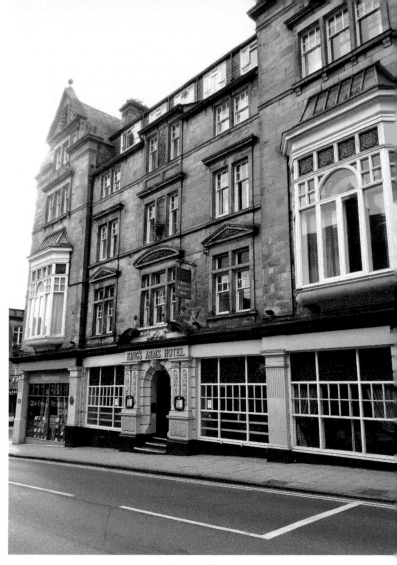

Right: Exterior of the
Royal Kings Arms.

Below: Carved
decoration around the
entrance.

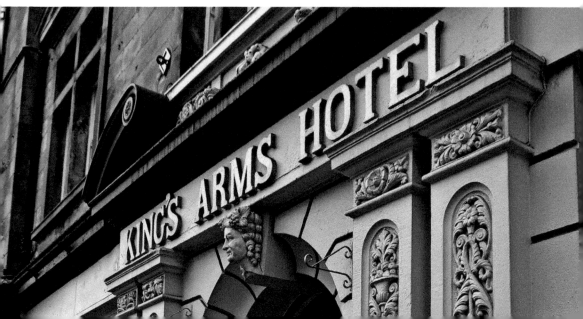

Collins and Charles Dickens, who mention the hotel in their joint story *The Lazy Tour of Two Idle Apprentices*, published in 1857.

Over the centuries, the hotel expanded into the adjoining buildings, giving the hotel its unusual layout. The old building was demolished between 1879 and 1882 and replaced with the current Victorian building, which can still be seen.

The new hotel offered its own horse-driven taxi service, which would pick up guests from the railway station, as well as offering stables for up to 100 horses. The hotel continued to serve guests throughout the twentieth century and is still one of the city's most popular historic hotels.

15. Penny's Almshouses

One of the city's smallest and least visited sites is Penny's Almshouses.

The first almshouses were established in 1485 by John Gardyner of Bailrigg, who left a sum of money in his will to provide accommodation for four people. Due to his generous inheritance, four men were housed at St Mary's Gate and were provided with a cash allowance for food and a maid.

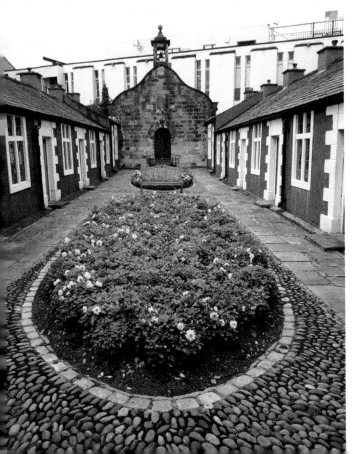

Interior courtyard.

Penny's Hospital, as it was known, came about through the bequest of William Penny, who left in his will a sum of money to enable the construction of almshouses for the 'poor indigent men and women within the town of Lancaster'.

The houses were built in 1720 and consisted of two rows of six houses opposite each other, with a central courtyard, chapel and arched entrance gateway. Above the archway is an inscription which records the good deed of William Penny and includes a warning in Latin telling people of ill repute to keep away. The residents not only received a house but were also provided with an allowance, set of clothes and the services of a chaplain.

The trustees of Penny's Hospital constructed The Assembly Room next to the almshouses in 1759 so that events could be held, and the money raised used to fund the charity. In 1860, Penny's Hospital became part of the Lancaster Charity, which brought together other small endowments within the city and now manages eight almshouse.

Between 1929 and 1930, King Street, where Penny's Hospital is located, was widened. The two houses nearest the road were demolished and replaced by two new ones located at the other end of the courtyard next to the chapel. The charity continues to serve residents of the local community to this day.

Exterior of the Almshouses with entrance gateway and carved dedication plaque.

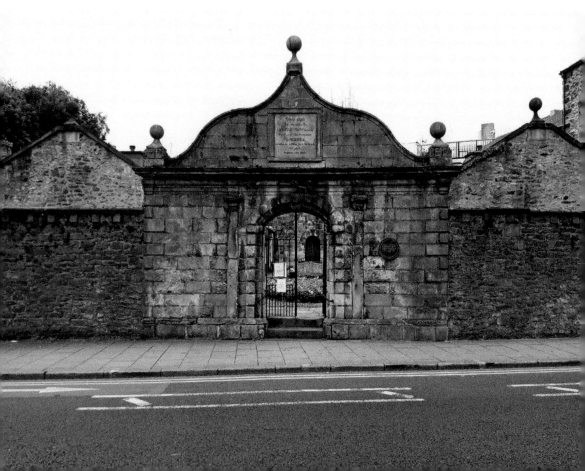

16. Atkinson's

One of the hidden gems in Lancaster is J. Atkinson & Co., which has been supplying the city's residents with tea and coffee since 1837.

In 1837, Quaker Thomas Atkinson founded the business J. Atkinson & Co., named after his wife Jane. He also opened the Grasshopper Tea Warehouse from which he sold tea, coffee, spices, refined sugar and chocolate.

Unusually, he used the logo of a grasshopper as a mark of quality on his goods, along with his slogan 'The Grasshopper only eats the Finest of Leaves'. Over the decades, the business continued to grow and prosper, becoming an important name in the town.

As Thomas and Jane grew older, their son, Thomas Atkinson junior, took over the running of the business, growing it and moving it from its first premises at No.1 Cheapside to a new warehouse on Castle Hill.

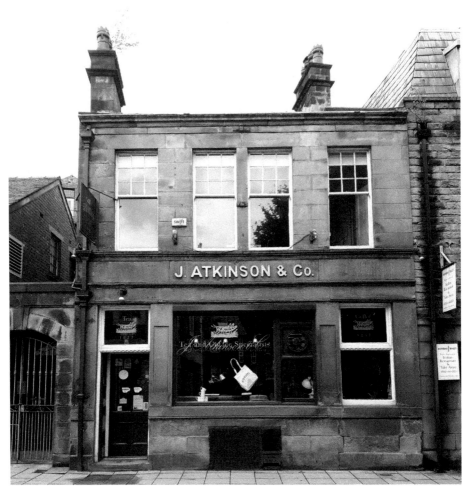

Exterior of Atkinson's.

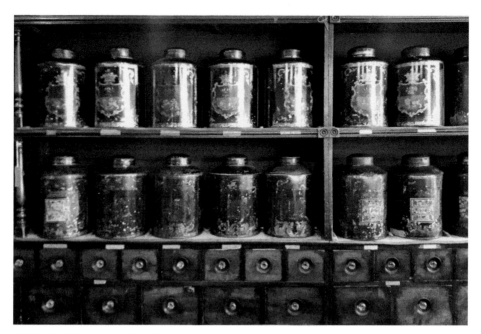

Shelves holding tea and coffee urns.

With the expansion of the town, the area around the warehouse was redeveloped and the original China Lane was demolished and widened to form China Street. In 1901 the business moved to its current premises on China Street.

The shop continues to sell tea and coffee, with its interior transporting visitors back to the past. The walls are covered with shelves holding original tea and coffee urns and coffee is still roasted in store using a vintage coffee roaster.

17. Paley and Austin Offices

On Castle Hill is arguably one of the most overlooked yet important buildings in the history of Lancaster.

This unassuming building was once the offices of Paley and Austin, the most famous architectural company in the city's history.

The history of the firm dates to 1835 when Edmund Sharpe established his architectural company on Penny Street. Over the following decades, the company expanded and was known by various names depending on the partners who were involved in the company.

In 1845, Sharpe was joined by Edward Graham Paley and the firm became known as Sharpe and Paley, with the company undertaking significant commissions including the new Lancaster Royal Grammar School and the remodelling of Hornby Castle. Paley officially retired from the business in 1851, although it continued to be known as Sharpe and Paley until 1856.

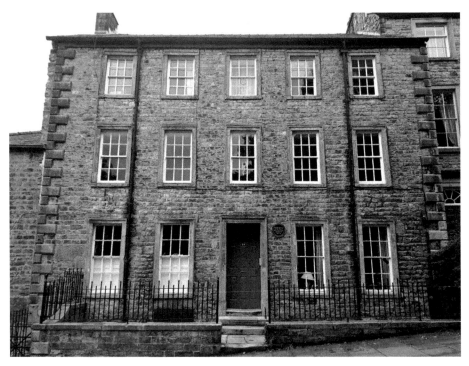

Exterior of the offices.

Sharpe continued to undertake commissions on his own, designing some of his most impressive buildings in Lancaster, including Lancaster Cathedral and the Royal Albert Hospital.

In 1867, Hubert Austin joined Paley as a partner, with the company becoming known as Paley and Austin and moving to their new offices on Castle Hill. Together they continued working on churches and grand houses, and in 1886, were joined by Henry Paley, the son of Edward. The practice then became known as Paley, Austin and Paley.

Edward Paley died in 1895 and the business became Austin and Paley, and over the next few decades various family members worked for the company. The business briefly became Austin, Paley and Austin in 1914 when Austin's son Geoffrey Langshaw became a partner; however, in 1915 he enlisted to serve in the King's Own Royal Lancaster Regiment and upon leaving the army in 1919 chose not to return to the business.

Hubert Austin died in 1915, after which time the business was solely controlled by Henry Paley, who continued to use the name Austin and Paley. By the 1940s, Henry Paley was wanting to retire and in 1945 the practice closed and records from the business were destroyed, with the offices sold to the Lancaster Corporation.

Henry Paley died a year later in April 1946, his passing signalling the end of one of the most significant and respected architectural practices in the north of England.

18. Shrigley and Hunt

One of Lancaster's overlooked businesses is stained glass company Shrigley and Hunt.

The origins of the business can be traced back to the 1750s when the painting and gilding company Shrigley's was founded. By the mid-nineteenth century, the company had changed hands and in 1868 fell under the control of Arthur Hunt.

Hunt was based in London and ran a successful stained glass and decorating company with a customer base primarily across the south of England. He had trained under the designer Henry Holiday at manufacturers Heaton, Butler & Bayne and was encouraged to create more realistic and brighter designs.

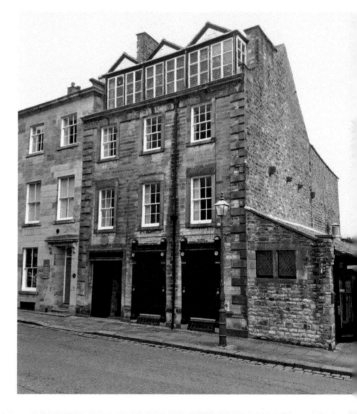

Right: Exterior of the old workshop.

Below: Original business signage visible below the skylights.

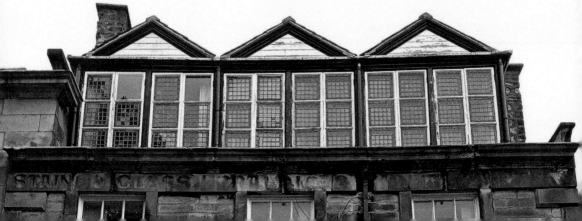

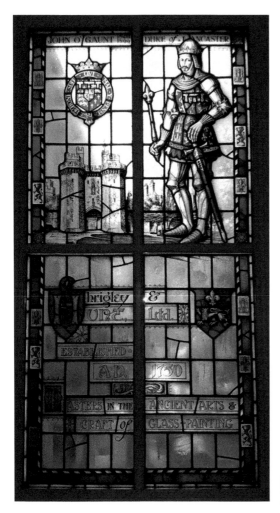

Example window panel depicting
John O'Gaunt.

In 1878, the business changed its name to Shrigley and Hunt and was based on
Castle Hill, with a showroom in London. Interestingly, during the late nineteenth
century, the business also created ceramic titles and decorative materials. At its
height the business was one of the leading designers and manufacturers of stained
glass in Britain, rivalling companies including William Morris & Co.

When Hunt died in 1917, the company was overseen by Joseph Fisher. After the
Second World War the business moved to a new location on West Road; however,
the site was devasted by a fire in 1973.

Joseph Fisher died in 1982, with the business also closing at the same time.
Today, the business is remembered for its remarkable windows, which can still be
seen throughout Lancaster and England, including at Lancaster Priory.

One of the finest examples of Shrigley and Hunt's work can be found at the
Lancaster City Museum in a window panel that depicts John O'Gaunt, designed
by E. L. Eaton.

19. Castle Hill Dispensary

On Castle Hill is located another of Lancaster's overlooked sites, a building of significance that tells the history of healthcare provision within the city. The Castle Hill Dispensary supplied healthcare provisions to the citizens of Lancaster between 1785 and 1832.

The physician Dr David Campbell moved to Lancaster in 1772 and became a well-respected member of the city. In 1781, a meeting was held in a local coffee house at which it was agreed to establish a dispensary in the town, located at Campbell's house on Castle Hill.

In 1785, largely due to his account, the new dispensary was built by public subscription to replace the earlier dispensary, also located on Castle Hill, close to where the later offices of Paley and Austin can be found.

The dispensary opened and was funded by donations, assisting residents who would otherwise be unable to pay for medical care. Dr Campbell served as the physician until 1805 when he was replaced by Dr Whalley and Dr Binn. Dr Campbell also researched and published an account of Lancaster's 1784 typhus epidemic, during which 500 people were infected, with 34 deaths. His report was one of the most detailed written at the time.

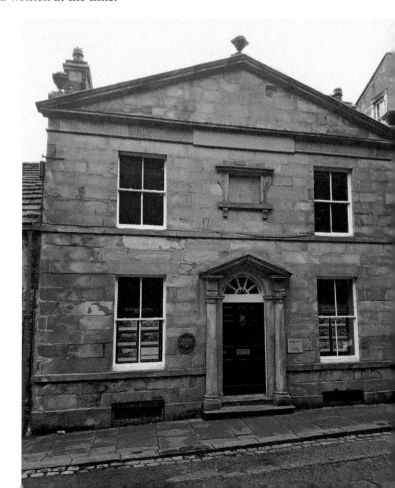

Exterior of the old dispensary.

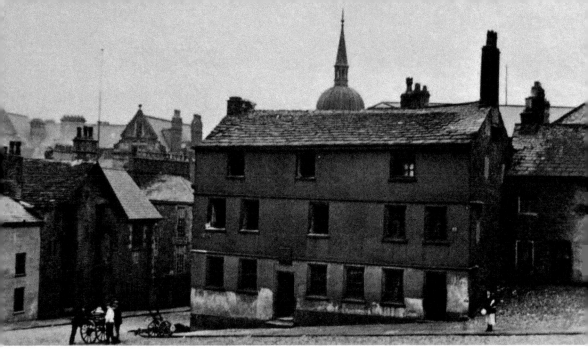

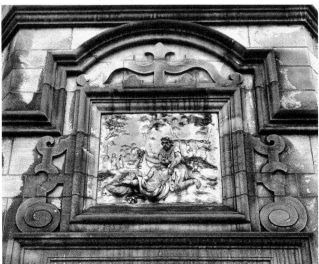

Above: Old photograph of the original dispensary.

Left: Carved plaque depicting the Good Samaritan.

Interestingly, the empty plaque above the doorway originally contained a relief of the Good Samaritan. It was removed and reinstalled above the entrance to the new Lancaster Royal Infirmary building when it opened in 1896.

20. Lancaster Castle

Another focal point on the Lancaster skyline is Lancaster Castle, which has an important history dating back to the Norman Conquest. Although the exact date of the foundation of the castle is unknown, it is believed that around 1090, Roger de Poitou, who was given the Honour of Lancaster, set about building a castle

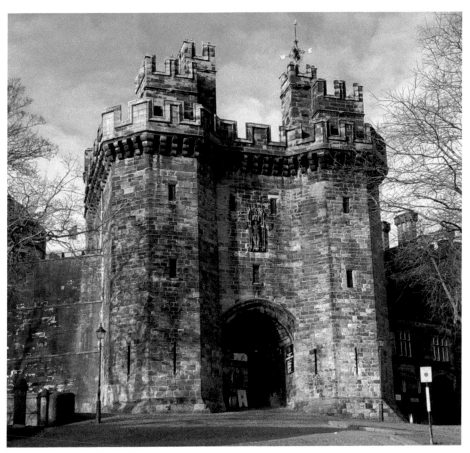

The gateway into the castle.

on the same site as the old Roman fort as well developing the town and later the priory. Unfortunately, he took part in an unsuccessful uprising against Henry I and in 1102 fled England, and his lands were confiscated.

Henry I gave the Honour of Lancaster to his nephew, Stephen of Blois, the future king. In 1139, Stephen and the Empress Matilda were at war over the English throne. Stephen gained control of the northern frontier by working with David I of Scotland, to whom he gave the Honour of Lancaster in 1141. When the war ended in 1153, an agreement was made that upon the death of Stephen, his throne would be taken by Henry Plantagenet, the son of Matilda. It was also decided that the title would be returned and given to Stephens son, William. In 1164, William died and the Honour of Lancaster came back into the possession of Henry II.

In 1189, Henry II died, and the Honour went to his son Richard the Lionheart who gave it to his brother John. Around this time, we also find the earliest evidence of the castle being used not only as a fortification but also as a place of imprisonment, with the earliest records dating to 1196.

Between the twelfth and thirteenth century, a huge rebuilding of castles took place across the country. John created a ditch outside the south and west walls and, later, Henry III constructed a gatehouse and curtain wall. When Henry IV became king in 1399, he built an impressive gatehouse, but after this period the main work undertaken was restoration and upkeep. Arguably the most important event in the history of the castle was the Pendle Witch Trials of 1612, with all the accused imprisoned and tried at the castle.

At the beginning of the Civil War, Lancaster was poorly garrisoned with only a small number of soldiers and was captured in February 1643 by Parliamentarian forces. The Royalists sent an army to try to retake the town with the town's outer defences collapsing in March 1643. Other attempts to retake the castle in April and June also failed. After the execution of King Charles I in 1649, the new government ordered the destruction of the castle with the exception of the jail and administrative buildings. The castle remained under the control of the Parliamentarians until the war ended in 1651. When monarchy was restored in 1660, King Charles II visited and ordered that every prisoner should be released. He was also petitioned to provide funding for the restoration the castle.

In 1786, Thomas Harrison was asked to create plans for renovations and additions to Lancaster Castle. Construction began in 1788 with the new Keepers House being completed first, followed by the Female Prison. Other buildings included the Male Prison, additional floors of accommodation for debtors, and an arcade around the south side of the keep providing shelter. He also incorporated new ideas into his designs, including the separation of male and female prisoners and by keeping debtors separate from criminals. One of the biggest developments was his design for the new Shire Hall.

Interior courtyard and buildings.

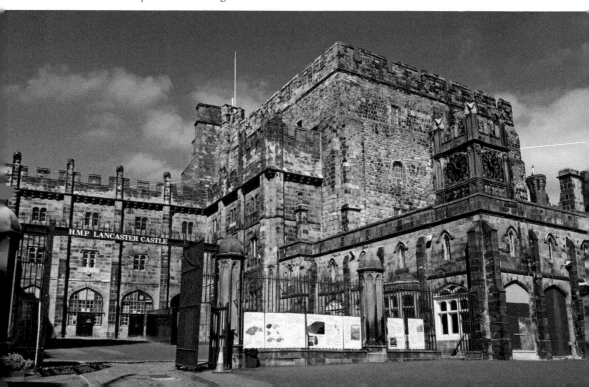

During the twentieth century, the castle's role in the community changed. The prison was closed due to low numbers in 1916; however, it was used to house German POWs during the First World War. Between 1931 and 1937 it was also used as a police training area, before reopening as a Category C prison for men in 1955. The prison finally closed in 2011 and is now used as a crown court. To this day, the reigning monarch also holds the title of Duke of Lancaster.

21. The Shire Hall, Lancaster Castle

One of the most unique features at Lancaster Castle is the striking and stately Shire Hall. In 1796, the medieval hall that was used to house the Crown Court was in need of modernisation and it was decided that it should be demolished.

Architect Thomas Harrison created plans for a new, modern Crown Court and Shire Hall. The most impressive feature in his plans was the Shire Hall that was completed in 1798. The Shire Hall was designed in an ornate Gothic style and contained detailed plasterwork and ornate carvings, including details such as the red rose of Lancashire.

Unfortunately, after the building was completed there was no money left, which led to a long delay in the completion of the interior decoration and furnishings. It was the architect Joseph Gandy who completed the interior works in 1802. His designs for the Shire Hall included window tracery and an elaborate Gothic canopy that sits above the judge's bench.

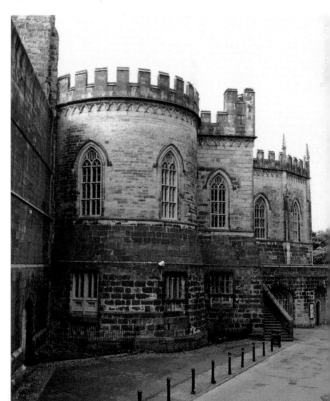

Exterior of the castle and the Hanging Corner.

Although the building was a modern development, it still had the character of its medieval predecessor. One of the most remarkable and impressive sites to this day is the wall of shields that holds the coat of arms of every English monarch since Richard The Lionheart, as well those of all the Constables of Lancaster Castle and the High Sheriffs of Lancashire.

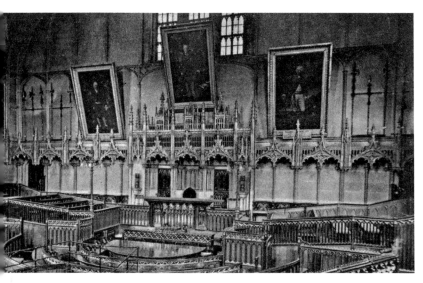

Left: Old photograph showing the interior.

Below: Exterior of the Shire Hall.

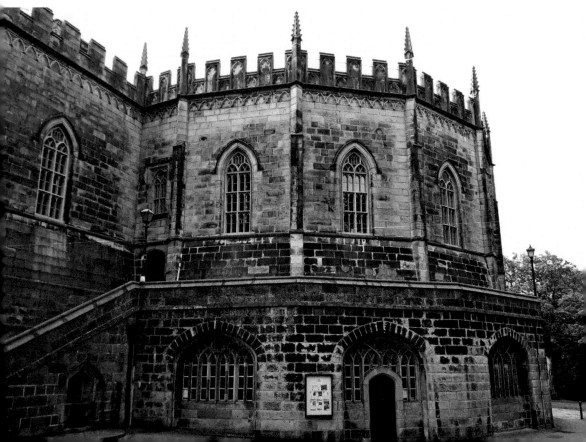

22. Lancaster Priory

Lancaster Priory, also known as the Priory Church of St Mary, is one of Lancaster's oldest buildings and has been overlooking the city from Castle Hill for over nine hundred years. It is located on the same site as the Roman fort that was constructed during the Roman occupation, and is also the location of an earlier Saxon Church built around AD 636.

The priory was the creation of Roger de Poitou who owned the Lordship of the area. It was established in 1094 as a Benedictine Priory dedicated to St Mary and part of the larger Abbey of St Martin of Sées in Normandy, France.

The church also had a close relationship with the Vatican. In 1133, the Abbot of Sées met with the Pope to discuss the collection of tithes and it was agreed that the Prior of Lancaster could collect taxes for the purchase of food for the resident monks.

In 1414, Henry V gave the management of the priory to the Bishop of Durham and it changed its allegiance to the Bridgettine Abbey of Syon in Middlesex. By 1430, the priory had become an important religious site within the district and became the official parish church.

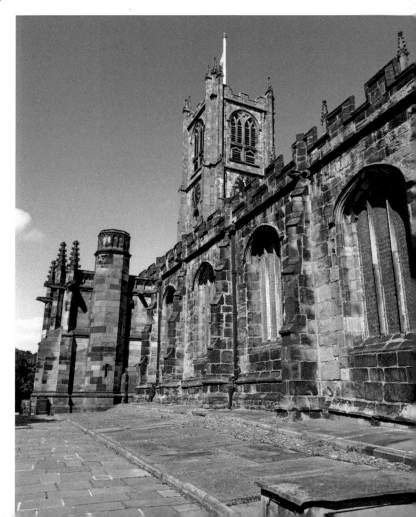

Exterior of the Priory building.

The biggest change in the history of the priory came about in 1534 when Henry VIII cut ties with the Catholic Church and made the reigning monarch the head of the Church, along with the rights to collect any taxes. In 1539, Henry VIII abolished the monastic institution at the priory, which brought to an end 445 years of monks living within the church.

The history of the church over the subsequent decades is relatively unknown, although we do know that in 1619 a Jacobean pulpit was erected, on top of which sat a carved bible and crown, and that in 1693 the two church bells were recast.

By the eighteenth century the church had fallen into a serious state of disrepair. In 1704, the churchyard had become so overcrowded that a charnel house was constructed to store the bones from old graves, which had been reopened to be reused. In 1743, the steeple was raised by 10 yards and its bells recast, but by 1753 the priory was once again in a poor state and the steeple was at risk of collapsing. It was decided to demolish and rebuild the tower. Henry Sephton was asked to design the new tower, which was completed in 1759 and can still be seen today.

The nineteenth century brought with it advancements in technology and the need for renovations. A new organ was installed between 1809 and 1811, and in 1847 the east window was installed. Gas lighting was also installed, which allowed the church to be lit properly without the use of candles for the first time.

In 1870, Paley and Austin undertook work on the chancel and also presented the priory with the famous eagle lectern that is still used today. Industrialist James Williamson donated £1,000 in 1885 to replace the bells and install a new clock on the tower.

The King's Own Regiment Memorial Chapel was constructed in 1903, and in 1912 an excavation discovered a possible Roman wall beneath the chancel and a small Saxon doorway in the west wall of the nave. In 1994, the church celebrated the 900th year since its foundation.

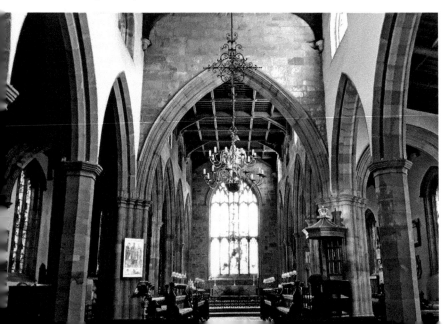

Interior of the Priory.

23. Roman Baths

Tucked away behind Lancaster Priory is the relatively unknown Roman Baths. The Romans first arrived in the North West around AD 71 and within a few years had complete control of the North.

The foundation of a Roman fort in Lancaster was likely at the request of Quintus Petillius Cerialis, who was the Roman governor of the province from AD 71-74. The site was undoubtedly chosen as it offered a clear vantage point of the area, with the River Lune, Morecambe Bay and surrounding land all visible from the fort.

From surviving records, we know that there were two units based in Lancaster during the first and second centuries. These were the Ala Gallorum Sebosiana and the Ala Augusta, both of which were cavalry (*ala*) units and it is believed that the number of soldiers in a cavalry unit was between 500 and 1,000 soldiers.

The first fortress to be constructed was built using wooden timbers and turf, but from surviving records we know that in AD 102 a new stone fort was built on the site. At the same time, a small village began to develop around the fort which housed the families of the soldiers garrisoned at the fort, as well industrial buildings, businesses and a market. We know that sometime within the next few decades the garrison had to move further north to assist with the expansion of the Roman Empire into Scotland.

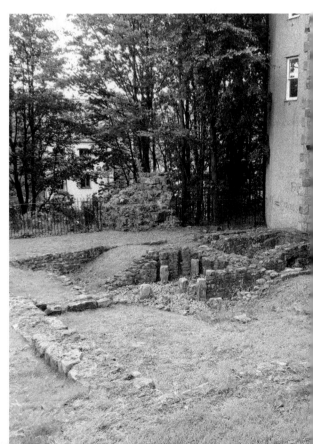

Excavated foundations of the Bathhouse and remains of the Wery Wall.

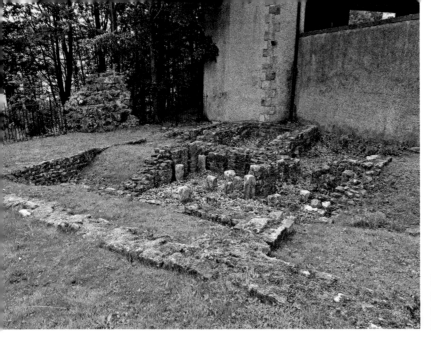

Foundations showing layout of the rooms and hypocaust.

Interestingly, the layout of the first Roman town in Lancaster can clearly be seen over 1,000 years later when we examine maps from the medieval period, with many of the original Roman roads and street layouts still in place. In around AD 250, the garrison returned to Lancaster and a third fort was built on the site. In addition to the new fort, the bathhouse was also constructed just outside the fort's northern extent.

Bathhouses were an incredibly popular Roman tradition and were used not only for hygiene but also as places to socialise and discuss business. From the evidence discovered around the site, it is believed that the bathhouse in Lancaster may have been part of a Roman hotel that was possibly used to accommodate visiting dignitaries and the upper class, with the building equipped with all the latest Roman luxuries and features.

From the excavated remains that can still be seen, the layout of two rooms, the caldarium (a sauna-like room with a hot plunge pool) and the tepidarium (a warm room used for relaxing between rooms), is visible. Over the decades, various excavations have uncovered other rooms in various states of preservation, as well as many artefacts, including pieces of painted plaster that show that the walls of the bathhouse would have been adorned with ornate painted decorations.

Around AD 330, the fort was rebuilt for the final time. During this period, the Roman Empire in Britain was stable with little unrest, although a new threat from Irish raiders was a concern. Due to this, the orientation of the fort was changed to face the River Lune, with the aim of spotting any incoming attackers at the earliest opportunity.

The fort remained in use until the early fifth century; however, after the fall of the Roman Empire the fort was abandoned. Today, in addition to the remains of the bathhouse, only a small fragment of the original fortress wall, known as the Wery Wall, survives.

24. The Judge's Lodgings

The Judge's Lodgings is the oldest existing townhouse in Lancaster, with evidence that the building is located on the site of a Roman kiln. Evidence of a wooden structure on the site dating to around 1314 has also been found and it has been suggested the building may have belonged to nobleman Robert de Holland.

The current building dates to around 1625 and was constructed using timber and materials from the original building on the site, including a stone fireplace dated to around 1550. The most important period in the history of the Judge's Lodgings came around the time that the house was owned and redeveloped by Thomas Covell.

Covell was well respected and held several important jobs in Lancaster. During his lifetime he acted as the town's mayor six times, as a magistrate and coroner, and even held the role of keeper of Lancaster Castle from 1591 to 1639, during which time he oversaw the imprisonment of the Pendle Witches. He also used the house to accommodate judges who were in Lancaster as part of the assize courts.

In 1662 the building was purchased by Thomas Cole, the Deputy Lieutenant of Lancashire. The building underwent significant alterations in 1675 and again in 1826. The use of the building by judges ended in 1975 and it was redeveloped into the Judge's Lodgings museum.

Nowadays, the museum is home to one of the most extensive collection of Gillows furniture, as well as a large collection of artworks, including the work of local artist George Romney who was born in Dalton-in-Furness.

Outside the Judge's Lodgings is the monumental Covell Cross. The cross was designed by local architects Paley and Austin and erected in 1903. Although known as the Covell Cross, it was built to commemorate the coronation of King Edward VII in 1902. Interestingly, the current cross stands on the site of an earlier ancient cross.

Below left: Exterior of the Judge's Lodgings.

Below right: The Covell Cross.

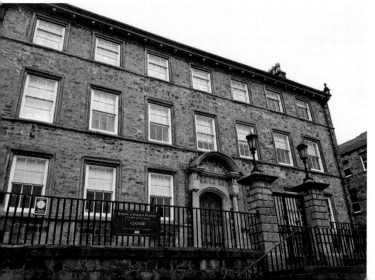

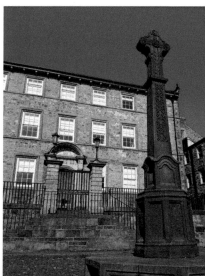

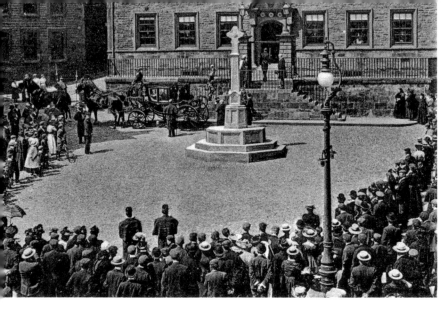

Old photograph of the building and cross.

25. The Sun Inn

Located on Church Street is The Sun Inn, one of the oldest pubs in Lancaster.

The current inn is located on the site of Lancaster's original Stoop Hall, a large medieval hall. The first record of the hall dates to 1680 when a licence was granted and four years later the licence was transferred, suggesting a change in ownership

In 1721, the inn was renamed The Sun Inn on Stoop Hall. The use of the word 'sun' in a pub's title was a popular way of honouring King Charles II after the strict regulations that were enforced during the reformation. This was the last time that Stoop Hall was used in its name; afterwards, the pub was always referred to as The Sun Inn.

There are also historical mentions of the inn dating from the Civil War. It is recorded in the diaries of Thomas Tyldesley, grandson of Royalist commander Sir Thomas Tyldesley, that he celebrated in The Sun Inn, with accounts of him enjoying an ale or two. In November 1745, generals from the Jacobean army stayed on their way to London and shortly afterwards on their return journey.

It had once housed a separate stable block, and in 1767 was recorded as also having a bowling green. In 1784, the Earl of Sefton sold the inn to the Carter brothers who redeveloped the surrounding area and created Sun Street. To do this, they demolished half of the original Sun Inn with the newly rebuilt inn opening in 1785.

Over the centuries, the inn was also used by many groups, including visiting judges from the assize court, the Port Commission from 1751 to 58, as well as the Freemasons. In 1812, the artist J. M. W. Turner stayed at the inn.

It is only since the mid-twentieth century that the inn has been referred to as The Sun Hotel as it now offers rooms, making it one of the oldest hotels in the city.

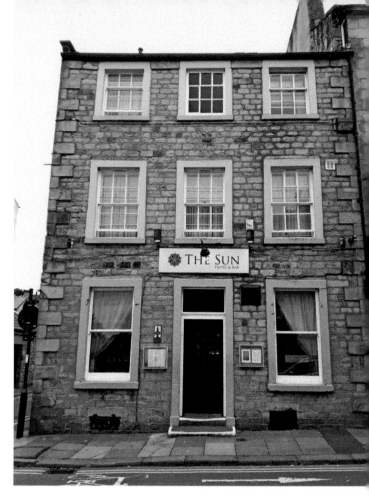

Right: Exterior of the Sun Inn.

Below: The building from Church Street.

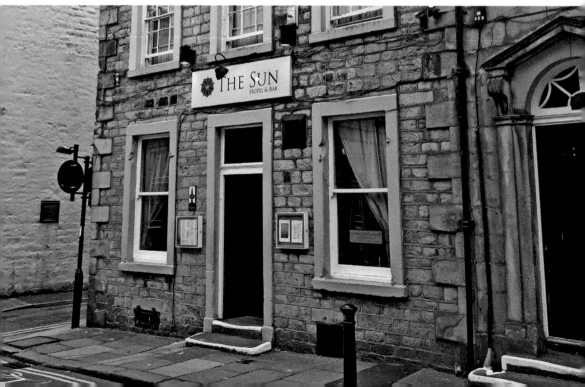

26. The Music Room

The Music Room is one of the city's least-known buildings and its early history is somewhat unknown.

The architect responsible for the design of the building is unknown, although it is known that the building was erected around 1730. It is believed to have been constructed as a garden pavilion for Oliver Marton, a lawyer who had made his fortune in London. From the surviving records we know that he lived at No.76 Church Street, which he purchased in 1723. He also owned a larger piece of land located behind The Sun Inn.

Despite the building's name, it was never used as a venue for music, but instead takes its name from the baroque plasterwork that adorns the walls and ceilings on the upper floor. This room is known as the 'Muses Room' and depicts the nine Muses who were the daughters of the Greek god Zeus and the goddess Mnemosyne.

The muses are considered to be inspirational goddesses and are Calliope (epic poetry), Clio (history), Erato (love poetry), Euterpe (music, song and lyrical poetry), Melpomene (tragedy), Polyhymnia (hymns), Terpsichore (dance), Thalia (comedy) and Urania (astronomy). Above the fireplace the god Apollo is represented, and the goddess Ceres is portrayed on the ceiling.

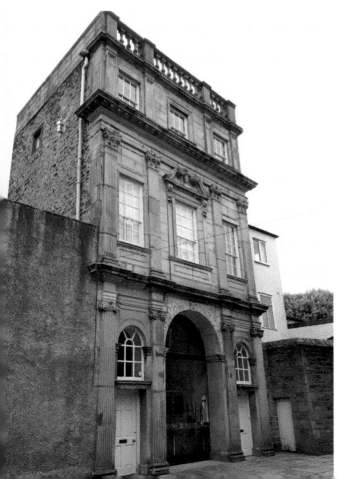

Exterior of the Music Room.

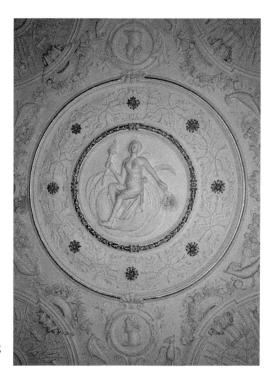

Interior plasterwork on ceiling depicting Ceres.

It is not known who designed and created the plasterwork, although it may have been Francesco Vassalli, who was known for the ornate stucco work that he had created at many grand homes around Lancashire during the 1730s. The upper floor offered guests a sheltered vantage point for viewing the formal gardens.

Oliver Marton died in 1744 and the building was passed on to his eldest son, Edward. When Edward died, childless, in 1758, the building and gardens were passed on to his brother, Reverend Dr Oliver Marton, who was owner of Capernwray Hall and a local vicar. Upon his death, the garden was sold for development and by the end of the eighteenth century several buildings had been erected on the land surrounding the Music Room.

Over the next century the building was owned by the Seward family, who had a successful business on Church Street. The Music Room, however, was poorly maintained and continued to fall into a poor state of repair. The Seward business went into liquidation in 1934 and the land was sold. In the 1950s the site was once again sold, and purchased by the Willans family, but by the 1970s the building was once again in a poor condition.

The Landmark Trust purchased the site and attempted to restore the building to its former glory. The façade was carefully cleaned and repaired and the roof was replaced. The interior of the building was in a state of neglect and the ornate decorations were at serious risk of being lost. The plasterwork was restored, with the process taking over six thousand hours to complete.

Since the restoration of the Music Hall it is now possible to stay in the upper rooms and the ground floor is currently used to house a small café.

27. The Old Town Hall

Located in Market Square is the majestic Old Town Hall building. It was designed by Major Thomas Jarrett and built between 1781 and 1783.

The building was constructed using local sandstone and is most iconic for its Tuscan-style portico. Originally, the ground floor was home to an open-air market where grain and butter was sold, but the openings in the walls were later changed and windows were installed.

In 1782, the prominent architect Thomas Harrison, who is best known for designing Skerton Bridge, designed an impressive cupola for the roof of the building. His design used a square-based structure, on top of which sits an octagonal section with the side that faces the square housing a clock face. The top section is made using a round drum decorated with Ionic columns and is capped by a dome.

The building underwent further modifications and extensions in 1871 and 1886, but by the beginning of the twentieth century the Lancaster Corporation who used the building had outgrown it and there was an urgent need for a new, larger town hall. In 1909, the New Town Hall was officially opened, signalling the end of the Old Town Hall as a government building.

Over the subsequent centuries the building was utilised for various purposes, including as a bank and town court house. Since 1923, it has been the home of Lancaster City Museum.

The museum today is well known for its archaeological collections and is home to many important local discoveries, including the Lancaster Roman Tombstone which was unearthed in 2005. The building has also housed the King's Own Royal Regiment Museum since 1929.

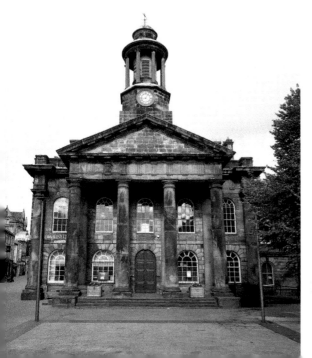

Exterior of the Old Town Hall building.

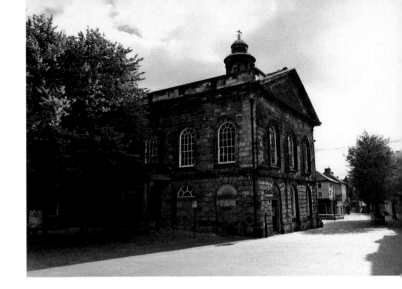

The back of the building looking towards Market Square.

28. St John's

Located to the south of the city centre is the rarely visited Church of St John the Evangelist.

The church was built in 1754–55 and is possibly the work of architect Henry Sephton. In 1784, architect Thomas Harrison was asked to design a new tower and spire for the church, which was paid for through the bequest of Thomas Bowes. The iron gates surrounding the church are original and date from 1818.

Originally, the church was a chapel of ease for the nearby St Mary's, based at Lancaster Priory. In 1842, it became a parish church due to the expansion of the town. The original organ dates to 1785 and sits within a mahogany casing built by local company Gillows, who also created a small communion table for the church.

Interestingly, the front pews on the south side were reserved for prominent members of the Lancaster Corporation, who contributed financially towards the construction of the church. Many local merchants provided their own donations to the building and its interior. The treble bell, located in the tower, is older than the church and was cast in 1747.

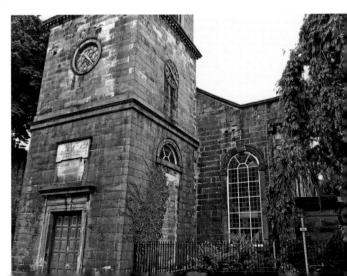

Exterior of the church.

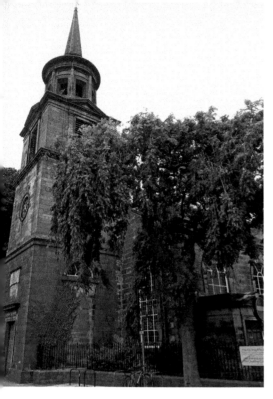

The tower and spire.

The graveyard is the resting place of many merchants who were involved in the North Atlantic slave trade, including John Lowther, John Nunns and Captain Greenwood.

During the 1870s, the south porch was built and in 1875 the three-deck pulpit was replaced by the current iron pulpit. The clock in the tower was installed slightly later in 1886. Around 1895, local stained glass manufacturers Shrigley and Hunt created the decorative windows in the north aisle.

Later, during the 1920s, a new chapel and vestry were added, and the interior of the church was restored by Sir Albert Richardson in 1955.

In 1958, the church merged with the church of St Anne and later closed its doors in 1981. Today the church is used as a local community hub and since 1983 has been under the guardianship of The Churches Conservation Trust.

29. The Gregson Baths

A unique and relatively unknown building in Lancaster is Lancaster Baths, also known as the Samuel Gregson Public Baths, on Cable Street.

In 1863, MP Samuel Gregson presented the first public baths to the city of Lancaster for use by the local population.

The building was relativity modest with some decorative elements giving the building a somewhat unique character through the mix of Tudor, Elizabethan and Italian-style features.

On the opening day, a procession, which included the High Sheriff of Lancashire and the Mayor of Liverpool, amongst many other officials and dignitaries, travelled from the Old Town Hall to the new baths. The streets were covered with colourful

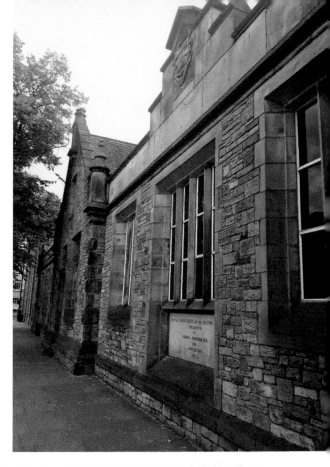

Right: Exterior of the old Gregson Baths.

Below: Carved dedication plaque.

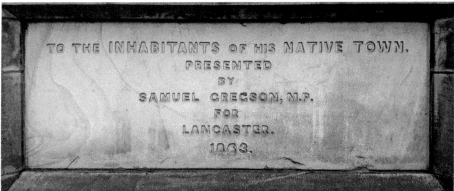

TO THE INHABITANTS OF HIS NATIVE TOWN,
PRESENTED
BY
SAMUEL GREGSON, M.P.
FOR
LANCASTER.
1863.

bunting and after the opening a grand dinner for 130 guests took place. The evening drew to a close with the singing of the national anthem, followed by fireworks.

With the completion of the new Kingsway Baths in 1939, the Gregson Baths were closed. From 1939 to 1983, the North Western Electricity Board occupied the building.

The later redevelopment of the site meant that the old baths needed to be demolished; however, it was decided that the original façade should be retained and rebuilt as part of the new supermarket. Each block was carefully removed and numbered, allowing it to be reconstructed later.

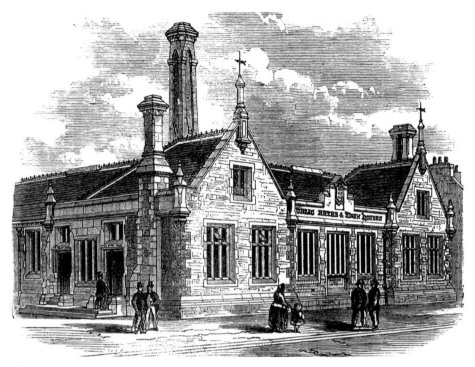

Old sketch of the original building.

30. Gillows of Lancaster

Gillows of Lancaster was one of the town's most prestigious businesses, with a long and illustrious history.

In 1730, Robert Gillow, who had made a name for himself in Lancaster as a joiner, house carpenter and furniture maker, decided to establish his business. The company relied on the exotic woods that were being imported as part of Britain's involvement in the North Atlantic slave trade. The first Gillows factory was located on Castle Hill.

By the 1740s, the business had shares in a ship called *Bridget*, which was used to import mahogany from the West Indies, with completed pieces of furniture returning to the West Indies to furnish the lavish houses on the plantations.

In 1757, Robert went into partnership with his son Richard, with the company name changing to Robert Gillow & Son. By 1768, Robert Gillow had left his share of the company to his other son, also named Robert. With the expansion of the company the brothers started to look further afield, and in 1769 opened a shop on Oxford Street in London.

In 1814, the Gillow family sold their business to the partnership of Redmayne, Whiteside & Ferguson. The business name was retained, and the company continued to expand, becoming the largest manufacturer of fine furniture outside

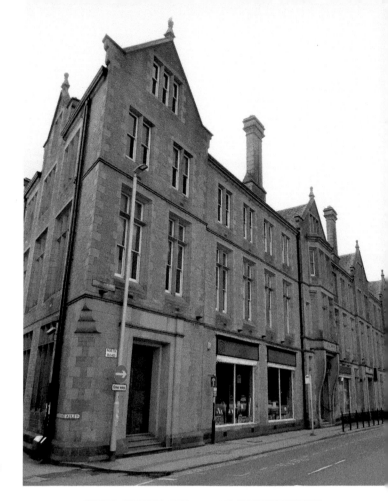

Right: Exterior of the old showroom.

Below: Carved detail above the doorway.

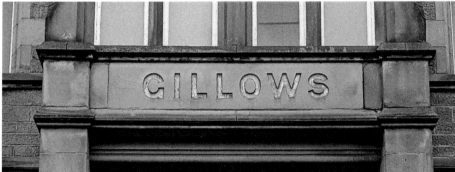

of London. They were so well reputed that they undertook commissions, furnishing many notable buildings around the world including in France, Germany and the United States. In 1878, a larger factory opened on St Leonard's Gate and their magnificent showroom on North Road opened three years later.

By 1897, the company was in severe financial difficulty and created an informal partnership with Warings of Liverpool, with Waring purchasing Gillows six years later, forming Waring & Gillows.

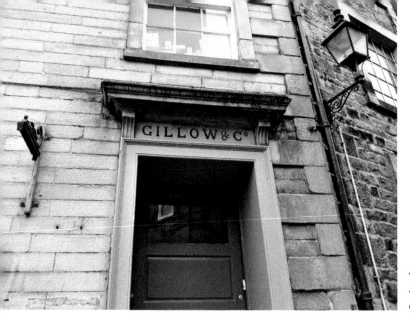

The original Gillows
workshop on
Castle Hill.

During the 1930s and 1940s, the company began to create interiors aboard luxury yachts and ships, including the *Queen Mary* in 1936 and the *Queen Elizabeth* in 1946. With the onset of the Second World War, their factory was tasked with producing propellers and ammunition chests, in addition to tents, trench covers and protective clothing.

The 1960s brought about a rapid decline in the business with the workshops in Lancaster closing in 1962. Today, the Gillow family is mostly known for being the owners of Leighton Hall, which is home to some notable pieces of Gillows furniture.

31. The Grand Theatre

The Grand Theatre is Lancaster's most famous and oldest theatrical venue, and the third oldest in Britain.

Construction of the theatre began in 1781, funded by subscription. It was opened a year later by Charles Edward Whitlock, the manager of several theatres around the North of England, and actor Joseph Austin. Upon opening, it was known simply as 'The Theatre, Lancaster'.

By the 1830s, the number of people visiting the theatre was on the decline and the venue was instead used as a meeting place for local societies, one of the most prominent being the Temperance Society.

In 1843, Edmund Sharpe bought the theatre and started a process of alterations to the building, which reopened as a music hall in 1849. The theatre closed again in 1882, reopening two years later under the name of the 'Athenaeum Theatre'.

Famous theatre architect Frank Matcham undertook modifications to the theatre, including the design of a new stage area in 1897; however, in 1908 the theatre suffered a catastrophic fire. It reopened the same year after a major refurbishment and was renamed 'The Grand Theatre'.

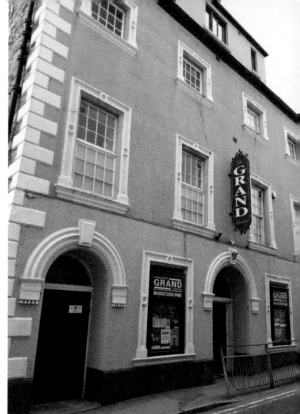

Right: Entrance to the theatre.

Below: Exterior of the theatre.

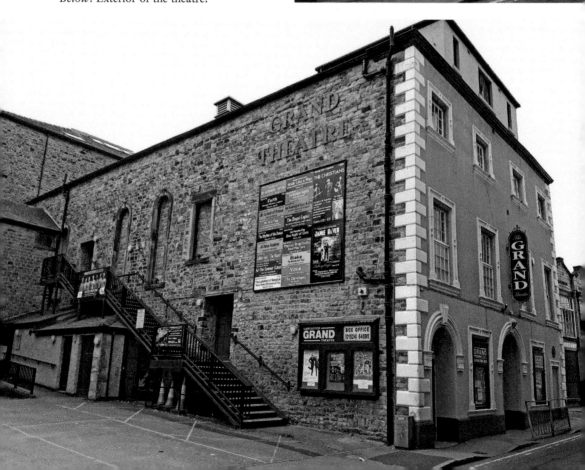

The Edwardian-style theatre that is visible today has barely changed since it was rebuilt after the fire in 1908. Over the decades, the building has also been used as a cinema, lecture theatre, bingo hall and museum.

Since 1951 it has operated as a charitable trust for the benefit of the local community, with plans to construct a modern extension fit for the twenty-first century in the pipeline.

32. Mitchells of Lancaster

Lancaster's oldest surviving brewery company is Mitchells of Lancaster, with a history dating back over 140 years.

In 1871, William Mitchell signed the lease for The Black Horse Inn and brewhouse. The brewery later moved to the new Central Brewery on Moor Lane during the early 1880s.

Another historic brewing company in Lancaster was Yates & Jackson Ltd., who were based at the Old Brewery on Brewery Lane. The company was established in 1669, and later purchased by John Proctor and William Jackson 1811. In 1984, the business was purchased by Daniel Thwaites & Co. Ltd. and their brewery was closed.

Daniel Thwaites & Co. Ltd was sold to Mitchells of Lancaster, who moved their manufacturing to the Old Brewery; however, Mitchells ceased brewing their own beer at the site in 1999. Mitchells purchased the York Brewery in 2008, and in 2016 sold eleven of their pubs and hotels to another business.

Today, Mitchells of Lancaster is still run by the same family and continues to be a well-known name in Lancaster, although the Old Brewery has been abandoned and is in a poor state of repair.

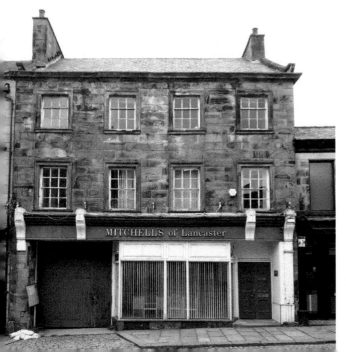

Offices on Moor Lane.

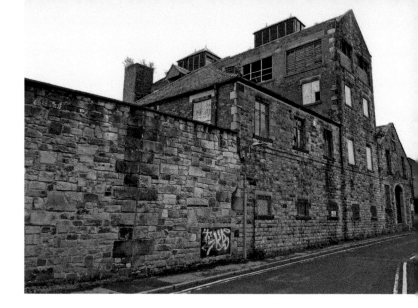

The Old Brewery
buildings.

33. The Dukes Theatre

Lancaster is now home to two theatres, the second being The Dukes.

The building occupied by The Dukes Theatre was originally constructed in 1796 as St Anne's Church, which continued to occupy the site into the twentieth century.

In 1971, the building reopened after an extensive refurbishment as a brand-new theatrical venue, with two auditoriums. The main Rake theatre is a traditional stepped design with a capacity of 313 people, whereas the more unusually arranged Round theatre offers a unique theatrical experience with a capacity of 240 people.

The theatre has become a creative hub within the local community and not only hosts theatrical productions, but also screens films and performs the popular yearly outdoor performance in Williamson Park.

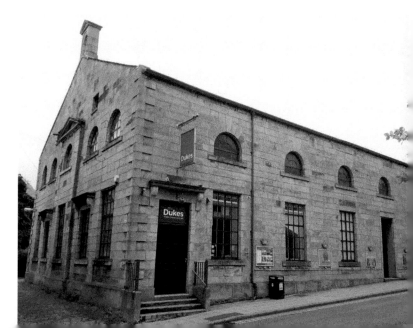

Exterior of the theatre.

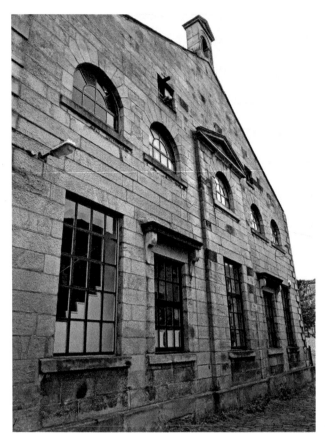

Carved details at the side of the building.

34. Palatine Hall

The Palatine Hall is one of Dalton Square's most overlooked buildings.

It was constructed as a Roman Catholic Mission in 1798–99, following on from various acts that were passed at the end of the eighteenth century allowing Catholics to freely practise their religion for the first time. It is possible that the building was designed by architect Robert Roper, who was responsible for building several churches around Lancashire. It was officially consecrated in 1799.

The church continued to serve the community until 1859, when the new St Peter's Church was officially opened and became the main Catholic place of worship in Lancaster.

After the church closed, the building was altered and over the decades was used as a Temperance Hall and the Hippodrome music hall. In 1931, the interior was remodelled into the County Cinema.

In 1983, the building underwent significant renovations. The interior was remodelled, taking into consideration the slope at the back of the building. After the renovations were complete, the building was used as council offices.

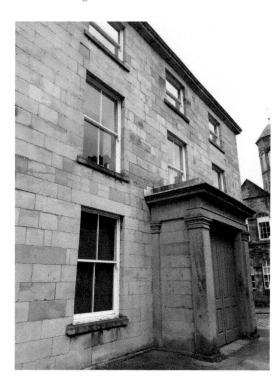

Right: Exterior of the Palatine Hall.

Below: Carved detail above the doorway.

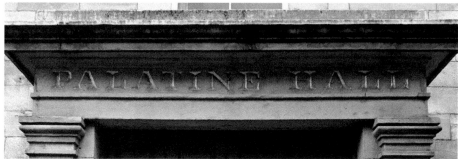

35. No.2 Dalton Square

Located in Dalton Square is the unassuming former house of Dr Buck Ruxton, a name that has almost been forgotten. The story of the murders was one of the most publicised cases of the 1930s and is best known for its revolutionary use of forensic science.

Dr Ruxton was born as Buktyar Rustomji Ratanji Hakim in 1899 and studied medicine at the University of Bombay. He emigrated to Edinburgh in 1927 and took a postgraduate course. He moved to Lancaster in 1930 to set up his business, and at the same time changed his name to the more English-sounding Buck Ruxton.

He lived in a large house at No.2 Dalton Square with his wife Isabella Kerr and their three children, Elizabeth, William and Diane. The couple had a stormy relationship and Isabella reported him to the police for assault. Isabella also attempted suicide in 1932 and left Ruxton for a short time in 1934. The events of 1935 and trial in 1936 not only shocked the town and nation, but also led to a grim end for this well-respected doctor.

On 14 September 1935, Isabella had arranged to meet her sisters in Blackpool to see the illuminations. She left Blackpool around 11.30pm and did not arrive home until the early hours of the morning. When she arrived home, the couple had an argument and he became violent, killing her in the process. The murder was witnessed by their maid, Mary Rogerson, who Ruxton also killed to try and hide his crime.

Ruxton dragged the bodies into the bathroom, drained the blood and finally dismembered and mutilated them. He wrapped up the pieces in newspaper, sheets and pillowcases and then had to find a place to dispose of them. On the night of 19 September he travelled to Scotland and disposed of the remains in a gorge near the town of Moffat in Dumfriesshire.

By 29 September, both women had been missing for a few weeks. Susan Johnson, who was travelling in Moffat, discovered the remains of an arm in the river. The police began searching the area and found thirty parcels containing human parts, which were examined by Professor John Glaister and Dr James Couper Brash, who attempted to reassemble the bodies utilising pioneering forensic techniques to identify the victims.

On 10 October, Ruxton was stopped at Lancaster railway station by Inspector Clark and claimed he had been to Edinburgh to try and find his wife. Around the same time,

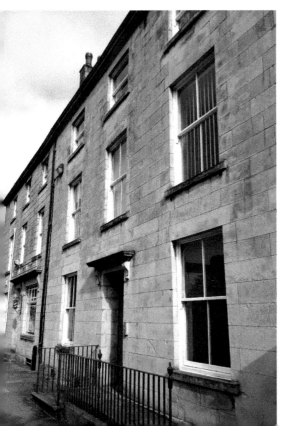

Exterior of the house.

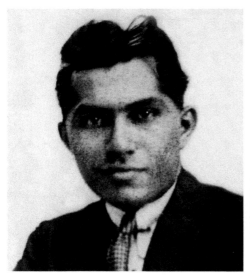 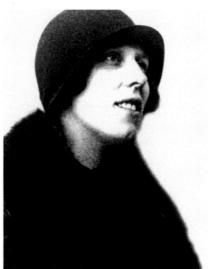

Above left: Buck Ruxton.

Above right: Isabella Ruxton.

Mary Rogerson's mother asked Ruxton for information about Mary, and reported her daughter as missing to the police. Isabella was also reported as missing by her family.

The police investigated and Ruxton was questioned; however, due to his reputation in Lancaster, his account that his wife had abandoned him after falling in love with someone else was believed to be true. Ruxton was once again brought in for questioning and formally charged with the murder of Mary on 13 October. On 5 November he was also charged with the murder of Isabella.

His method of disposal led to his own demise as the paper that he wrapped some of the body parts in included a special edition of the *Sunday Graphic* from 15 September, which was only sold in Morecambe and Lancaster. Upon searching his house, bloodstains were also discovered.

He was imprisoned until his trial, which began on 2 March 1936. He was found guilty and sentenced to death for his crimes on 13 March, after which he was executed by hanging at HMP Manchester on 12 May, overseen by executioner Thomas Pierrepoint.

36. The New Town Hall

The most prominent building in Dalton Square is the New Town Hall.

By the beginning of the twentieth century the Old Town Hall, located in Market Square, was unable to fulfil the growing needs of the city council and in 1904 a committee was formed to draw up the plans and requirements for a new town hall.

The process involved the committee visiting many buildings throughout England to finalise its list of requirements for the new building. Some of the most

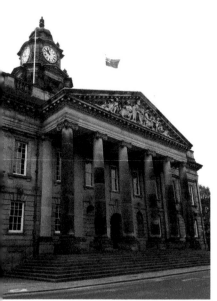 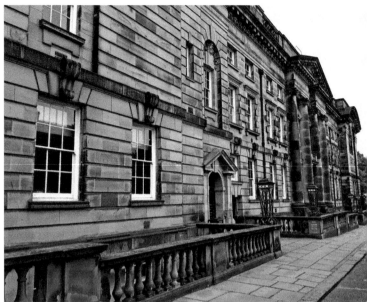

Above left: Exterior of the new Town Hall from Dalton Square.

Above right: The side of the Town Hall close to the War Memorial.

notable buildings the committee visited were designed by architect E. W. Mountfield, who had previously designed Sheffield Town Hall and The Old Bailey in London.

The committee asked him to draw up plans and designs for Lancaster's new Town Hall. Unfortunately, the corporation was unable to finance the new building and local industrialist Lord Ashton offered to pay for the construction himself.

Construction of the building began in 1906 and was completed three years later in 1909. Importantly, many local businesses were involved in the process, including Gillows, who were responsible for the stonework, woodwork and furniture, and Shrigley and Hunt, who created the striking stained-glass windows. The construction cost £155,000, which also included the redevelopment of Dalton Square and the erection of the statue of Queen Victoria.

The Lancaster War Memorial is located in a small garden to the side of the Town Hall and commemorates the lives of soldiers lost in battle.

37. St Peter's

One of the city's tallest buildings is The Cathedral Church of St Peter, also known as Lancaster Cathedral.

The history of the Catholic church in Lancaster can be traced back to 1799, when the first Roman Catholic Mission was opened in Dalton Square.

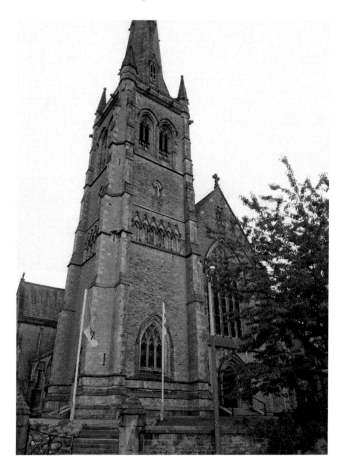

The church tower.

By the 1850s, the number of worshippers had grown to the extent that the current building could no longer support their needs and a new church was urgently needed.

In 1857, the foundation stone was laid for the new St Peter's Church, designed by local architect Edward Paley, who had previously designed a new presbytery, convent and school on the site. The cathedral cost £15,000 and officially opened on 4 October 1859. It was consecrated by the Bishop of Liverpool, Dr Alexander Goss.

Over the following decades the building underwent several alterations by architects Paley, Austin and Paley. These included a new font in 1860, organ gallery in 1888, chancel stalls in 1899, and in 1901 a new baptistry at a cost of £4,000.

In 1909, the church celebrated its Golden Jubilee and underwent alterations overseen by architect Giles Gilbert Scott. These included a new marble floor, replacement of the old pine benches with oak pews, and the construction of a new altar.

The Diocese of Lancaster was created in 1924 and the church was elevated to the status of cathedral. The church celebrated its centenary in 1959 and underwent further refurbishments, followed in 1995 with the restructuring of the east end of the church by Francis Roberts.

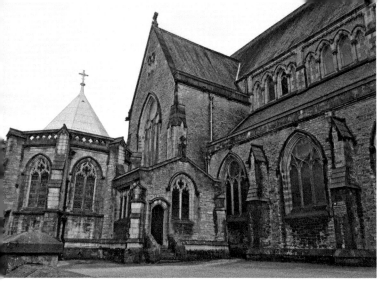

The side of the church from East Road.

38. St Thomas'

Another of Lancaster's forgotten buildings is St Thomas' church, located a short distance away from the Town Hall.

The church was constructed by subscription in 1840–41 and designed by Edmund Sharpe. It was built on land donated by George Marton of Capernwray Hall. Other

Below left: Exterior of the church.

Below right: The church tower.

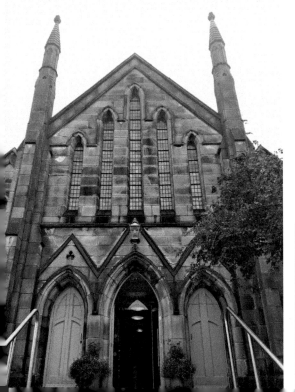

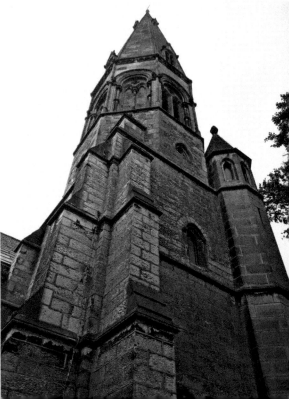

benefactors included Elizabeth Salisbury, who gave £1100 and Queen Victoria, who donated £150 in her role as the Duke of Lancaster.

It was officially consecrated on 14 June 1841 by John Bird Sumner, the Bishop of Chester. The first vicar was Joseph Armytage, who took up the position from 1841 until 1845. He was succeeded by Reverend Colin Campbell.

St Thomas' School, next to the church, was built in 1843. In 1852–1853, Edward Paley designed the steeple and the chancel. The organ was built by John Banfield in 1852 and later rebuilt in the 1880s by Richard Tubbs.

39. Springfield Barracks

In 1856, a new barracks, known as Springfield Barracks, was constructed for the 1st Royal Lancashire Militia and the building was designed by local architect Edmund Sharpe. It was named after the hall and estate that was purchased in order to build the Lancaster Royal Infirmary.

Within a few years they moved to a new, larger site. In 1883, the 1st Royal Lancashire Militia became the 3rd and 4th Militia Battalions of the King's Own Royal Lancaster Regiment.

They moved to the larger Bowerham Barracks, which provided more suitable accommodation and facilities, including accommodation for officers and sergeants and their wives, as well as stables, an armoury and a hospital.

The site was later taken over by Storey Brothers & Co. as part of their White Cross site.

Exterior of the old Barracks.

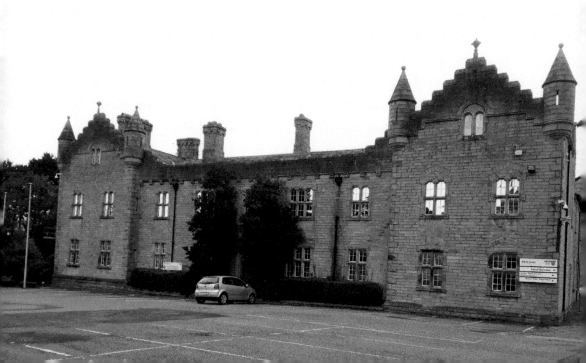

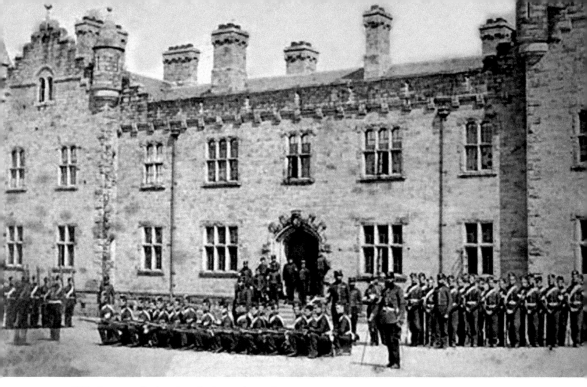

Old photograph showing the barracks and troops.

4c. White Cross

The mills along the side of the canal give an insight into Lancaster's important industrial past, which stretches back to the opening of the Lancaster Canal in 1797.

Before the introduction of the railways to Lancaster in 1840, the only way of transporting goods was by barge.

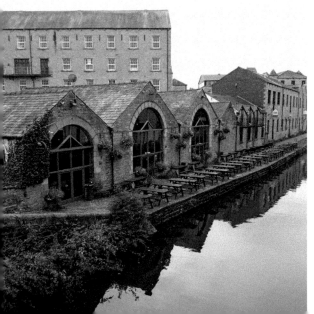

The warehouses and buildings.

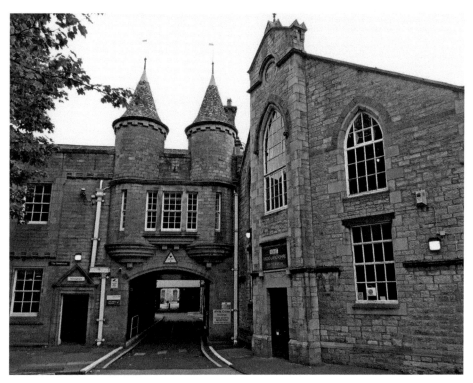

Entrance gateway to White Cross.

The oldest mill in Lancaster is White Cross Mill and dates to 1802. It was constructed as a cotton mill and was one of the first to be powered by steam. It was owned by Thomas Mason until 1827, when it was taken over by George Burrow and Thomas Housman Higgin.

In 1849, Storey Brothers & Co. was founded by Thomas, Edward and William Storey and Edmund Sharpe for the manufacture of table baize, also known as American cloth.

As the cotton industry began to decline during the mid-nineteenth century, the mill was resold before being purchased in 1856 by Storey Brothers & Co. and refitted for the manufacture of oilcloth. In 1861, a fire seriously damaged the mill, with most of it needing to be rebuilt.

This side of the canal was also home to several other mills that were purchased by Storeys, including Moor Lane North Mill, Moor Lane South Mill and Queen's Mill, which was demolished in 1983. The original Springfield Barracks building served as the offices of the business.

Most of the mills survived into the late twentieth century until some were demolished, with the remaining mills continuing to operate. During the late 1980s, the White Cross site underwent a significant regeneration, with the old factory buildings and warehouse being restored for use as offices, an adult college and a pub.

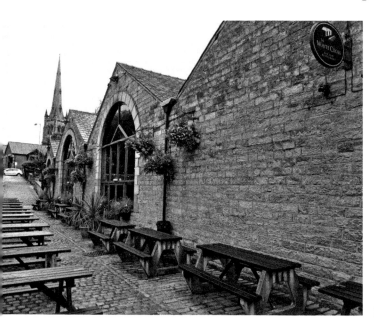

Exterior of the old warehouses.

41. Ripley Hospital

One of the more overlooked buildings in Lancaster is the Ripley Hospital, now known as Ripley St Thomas school.

The history of the school and its founders can be traced all the way back to 1791 when Thomas Ripley was born. Later, Thomas Ripley became a merchant

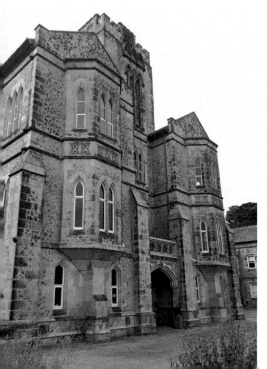

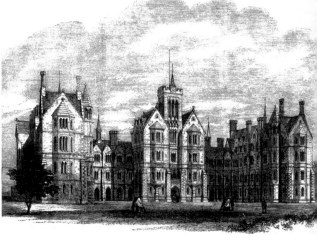

Above: Exterior of the main building.

Left: Old sketch of the hospital.

who traded out of the ports of Liverpool and Lancaster and was one of the first English merchants to trade with China before focusing on trade with the West Indies.

As Ripley made his fortune, he was keen to establish a charitable hospital modelled on the Liverpool Blue Coat School, partly influenced by the fact that he and his wife Julia were childless. On his death in 1852, he left a large sum of money in his will with the aim of establishing a hospital for fatherless children, particularly children whose fathers had been lost at sea.

Julia purchased the Springfield Estate to be used as the location for the new hospital and at the same time she moved into Springfield Hall on the estate, where she lived until her death in 1881.

The school opened in 1864 and catered for both boys and girls equally, with 300 pupils attending. To be considered, pupils had to live within 15 miles of Lancaster Priory or 7 miles of Liverpool Cathedral.

Ripley Hospital continued to operate until the start of the Second World War when it was requisitioned as part of the war effort, with the pupils transferring to Capernwray Hall, close to Carnforth. After the war, the school was requisitioned for another three years and used as a training college for teachers.

The church on the site.

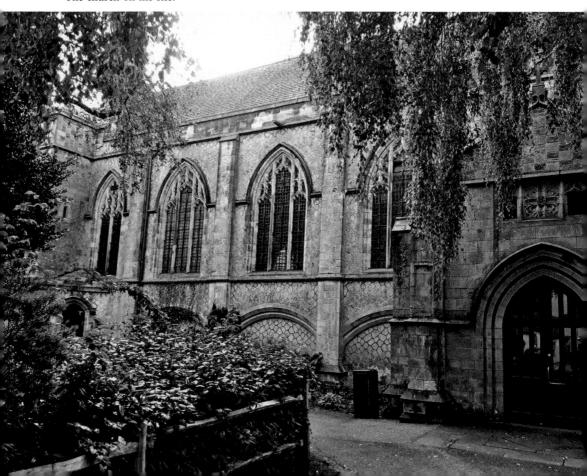

Once the teachers left, the school became a National School, followed by a boys' secondary school, and in 1966 the Ripley Boys' and St Thomas Girls' schools merged to become the Ripley St Thomas School.

42. Royal Lancaster Infirmary

For over one hundred years, the Royal Lancaster Infirmary has been the primary medical establishment serving the city and its residents.

The story of medical institutions in Lancaster can be traced back to the original dispensaries around Castle Hill and, later, Fever Hospital, which was built in 1815. These two institutions eventually amalgamated and relocated to Thurnham Street in 1833.

The building was designed by local architects Paley and Austin and is located on part of the land that formed the Springfield Estate, with Springfield Hall as its main residence. The hall was built around 1792 by James Hargreaves and later occupied by Julia Ripley, who founded the Ripley Hospital.

The hospital was constructed between 1888 and 1896, and funded by subscription. It was officially opened by the Duke and Duchess of York on 24 March 1896. In 1929, the hospital underwent alterations and extensions and over the decades has expanded further.

The original hospital building has some unusual design features, from its carved stonework to the prominent octagonal tower featuring the relief of the Good Samaritan, which was relocated from the Castle Hill Dispensary.

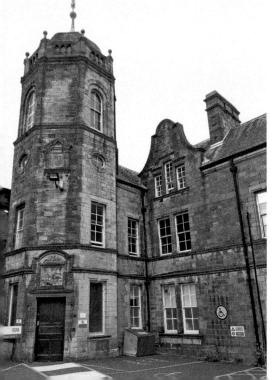

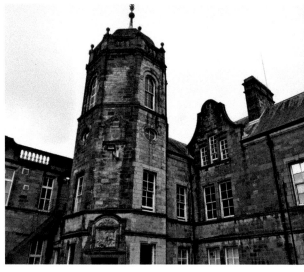

Above: Exterior of the original buildings.

Left: The prominent tower.

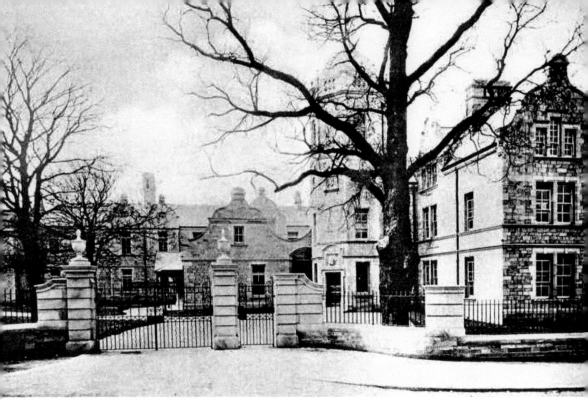

Old photograph of the hospital.

The site also occupies the former terminus station of the Lancaster and Preston Junction Railway, which closed in 1846. Today, the hospital continues to serve the residents of Lancaster and the wider community.

43. Lancaster (Greaves) Railway Station

When we think of Lancaster and its railways today, we see only a small part of the city's history.

Lancaster was first served by a railway known as the Lancaster and Preston Junction Railway, which connected Preston with the new terminus station in Greaves, close to the present-day Royal Lancaster Infirmary.

It is sometimes identified as Lancaster (Penny Street) Railway Station, although upon opening was known simply as Lancaster Railway Station, as there were no other stations.

The railway was in operation from 1840 until 1849. It opened on 26 June 1840, with the building designed by Edwin Gwyther and used as the headquarters of the railway company. It was replaced by the new Lancaster (Castle) Railway Station, which opened in 1846.

When the Lancaster (Castle) Railway Station opened in September 1846, the new railway line was connected to the Lancaster and Preston Junction Railway to the south of Lancaster. In 1849, the Lancaster and Carlisle Railway leased the original junction line and closed the Greaves station to passengers.

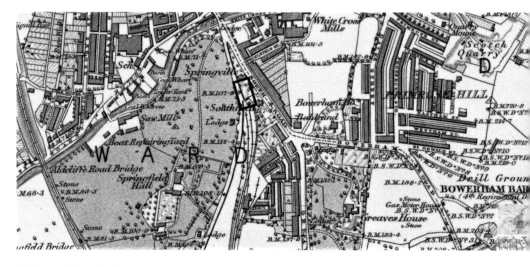

Above: Old OS Map with the location of the old station marked.

Left: The old station building.

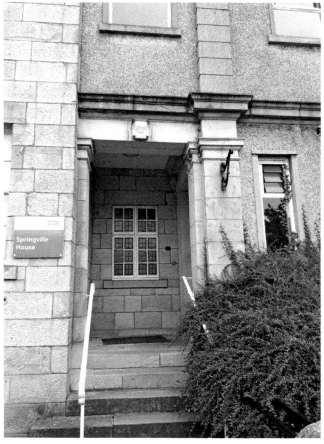

The railway line was amalgamated into the Lancaster and Carlisle Railway in 1859, and in 1879 became part of the London and North Western Railway, with the line used for freight until the mid-twentieth century. Today, the building remains and is part of the Royal Lancaster Infirmary.

44. Bowerham Barracks

One of Lancaster's hidden buildings can be found in Bowerham, on the current site of the University of Cumbria, close to Williamson Park.

In 1873, The War Office decided that they needed to build a new barracks to house the King's Own Royal Lancaster Regiment. They purchased some land on the Bowerham Estate for £7300 and between 1876 and 1880 constructed the new base, complete with accommodation for soldiers, an armoury and stable blocks.

On 20 April 1880, a group of thirty troops first lodged at the new Bowerham Barracks, followed by more soldiers in the May and June of 1880. Three years later, the 1st Royal Lancashire Militia became the 3rd and 4th Militia Battalions of the King's Own Royal Lancaster Regiment and moved to the new site.

The main use of the Bowerham Barracks was as a Regimental Depot, providing new recruits with their basic training between 1880 and 1959. During the Second World War, the Auxiliary Training Service was stationed at the barracks. At the end of the war, the King's Own Royal Lancaster Regiment was merged with the Border Regiment, which resulted in the closing of the barracks in 1959.

The Lancaster College of Education took over the site in 1962 with the first students arriving two years later, and the college becoming known as St Martin's College. In 2007, St Martin's merged with several other institutions to form the University of Cumbria.

Old photograph of the barracks.

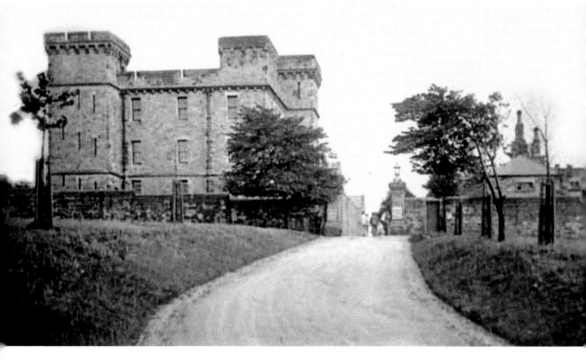

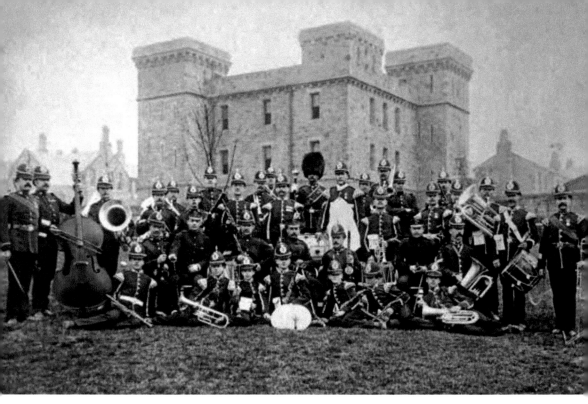

Old photograph showing the barracks and troops.

45. The Greg Observatory

One of the city's most remarkable buildings once stood on a prominent hilltop within the grounds of Williamson Park, with a history that goes all the way back to the Georgian Period and Lancaster's port.

As the slave trade began to decline, people began to look for new opportunities and the expansion of the British Empire provided new prospects. The cotton industry was beginning to take hold and some wealthy local businessmen wanted to invest their money in new industries.

One of the most notable was Isaac Hodgson, who set about constructing Low Mill in Caton, which began production in 1784. By 1817, the mill had been transferred to John Greg, due to a debt that was owed. The business grew, and additional buildings were constructed in Lancaster on Moor Lane. At the same time, advancements in technology allowed steam-powered machinery to be installed at Low Mill.

John became wealthy and built a large country house at Escowbeck Cottage in Caton. He also developed an interest in science. He purchased a 7.5-inch reflecting telescope, astronomical clock and transit telescope, and constructed an observatory in the grounds of the house.

When John died in 1882, his son Albert was unsure as to what to do with his father's belongings and offered to donate the equipment to the town.

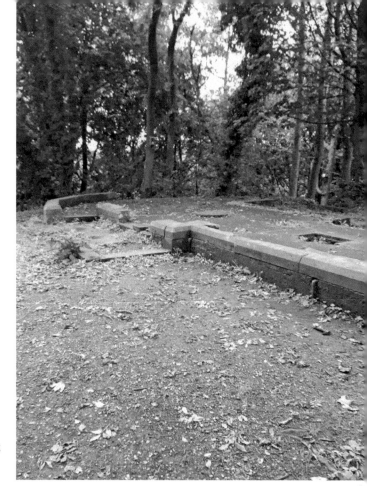

Right: The remains of the old observatory.

Below: Old photograph showing Williamson Park and the Greg Observatory.

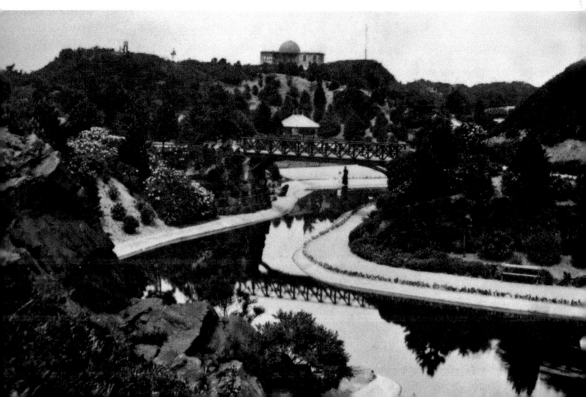

He approached the Lancaster Corporation with his offer but due to the high maintenance costs it took almost ten years for them to reach a decision. The observatory finally opened in 1892.

The observatory was looked after by curator George Ingall, who charged visitors one penny to see the observatory. Evening lectures were given by Reverend John Bone. It was also possible for esteemed visitors to request the keys to the observatory overnight, allowing them access once the park had closed to the public.

By 1905, Ingall had retired and was replaced by James Dowbiggin who had been involved in taking and reporting weather readings for the area from the nearby weather station. Every year there was an inspection by the Meteorological Office, which ensured that the equipment was well maintained, as well as checked if the records were thoroughly completed. In 1939, the weather station failed its inspection and James Dowbiggin retired due to poor health.

The Lancaster Corporation had to find a new custodian quickly, but the main problem was that the curator's salary was only 10*d*, in addition to the penny admission per visitor. A radical solution was needed, and they approached the Lancaster Royal Grammar School, which agreed to the day-to-day running of the observatory. The outbreak of the Second World War meant that many teachers were called up to serve and their responsibilities were to pass on to the senior pupils. During this period, the pupils faced many mechanical issues and problems with maintenance.

By 1944, the observatory was in a poor state and the telescope was in serious need of repair. Due to the ongoing war and the weather station failing its inspection, the observatory was closed and abandoned. During the 1960s the remaining equipment was scrapped, and the remaining parts of the building were demolished. Only the foundations survive today.

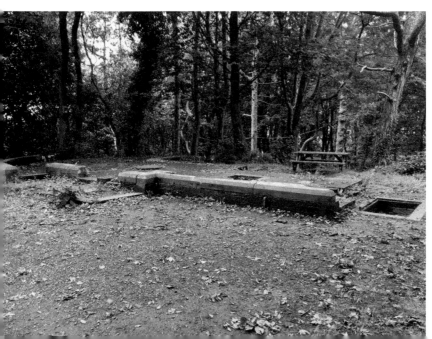

Foundations showing layout of the rooms.

46. Ashton Memorial

Ashton Memorial is one of Lancaster's most famous and prominent landmarks and has been part of the skyline for over 100 years. The history of the building can be traced back to the prominent Williamson family, who were instrumental in creating Williamson Park in the 1870s.

James Williamson junior was the third of the four children of James Williamson senior, a Lancaster businessman who ran a linoleum and oilcloth company. After studying at the Lancaster Royal Grammar School, he began working in the family business and eventually took over the management of the company in 1875. He expanded the company, making himself a multimillionaire and earning himself the title 'Lino King'.

He donated the park to the Lancaster Corporation in 1881, and it was formally opened for public use in 1896. At the beginning of the twentieth century, Sir John Belcher was commissioned to improve the park and designed a fountain, temple and imposing Palm House.

In 1907, Williamson asked Sir John Belcher to design a monument within the park. It was originally intended as a memorial for his deceased second wife, but by the time it was completed in 1909, he was remarried for a third time to Florence Maud Whalley.

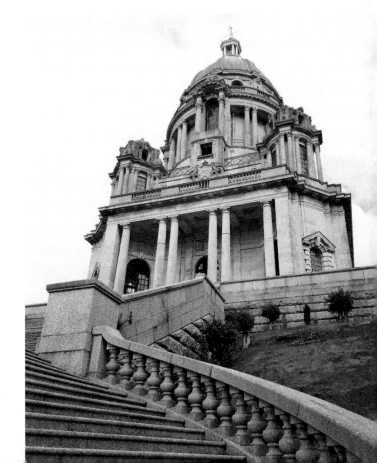

Exterior of Ashton Memorial.

Gillows of Lancaster were the main contractors of the monument; however, from the start of construction there were many issues that needed resolving. The final cost of the building is estimated to be around £87,000.

The building was originally to be constructed solely from stone; however, as the costs increased, the builders began to use cheaper materials and new methods of construction. They used steel girders to take the weight of the building and used concrete, which was later clad in stone to provide the desired look.

These changes to the construction led to many serious structural issues over the subsequent decades. Within the first decade, water had begun to seep into the fabric of the building, causing the internal steelwork to rust and the concrete to crack. The building was in such a poor state by the 1920s that Williamson provided funding for repairs, which was continued by his wife after his death in 1930.

In 1962, the building suffered a serious fire and by 1981 it had become structurally unsafe and was closed. A fundraising appeal was launched to raise the estimated £600,000 to restore the building. Repairs were undertaken between 1985 and 1987. Ashton Memorial was officially reopened in May 1987 and today is one of Lancaster's most iconic buildings.

The memorial and surrounding landscape.

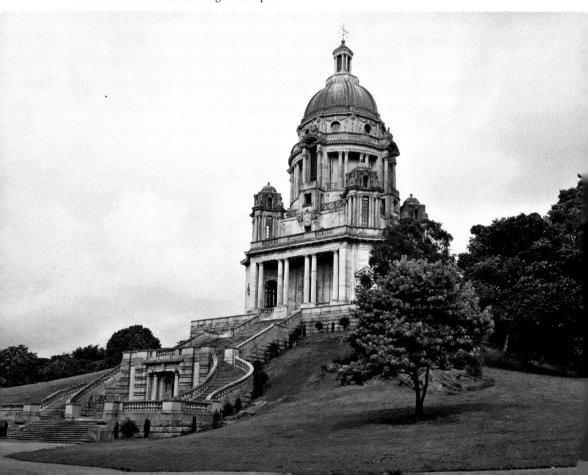

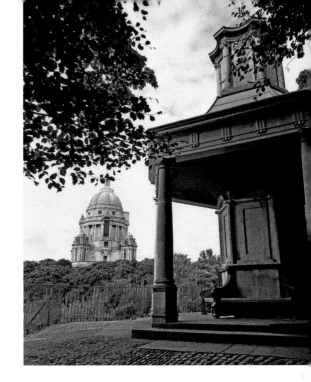

The folly and memorial.

47. Lancaster Royal Grammar School

One of Lancaster's oldest establishments is the Lancaster Royal Grammar School, with a history dating back almost 800 years.

The school was first founded between 1235 and 1256 and later endowed by John Gardyner of Bailrigg.

Old sketch of the original school building.

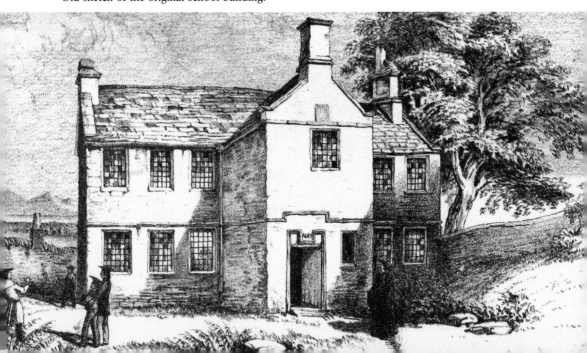

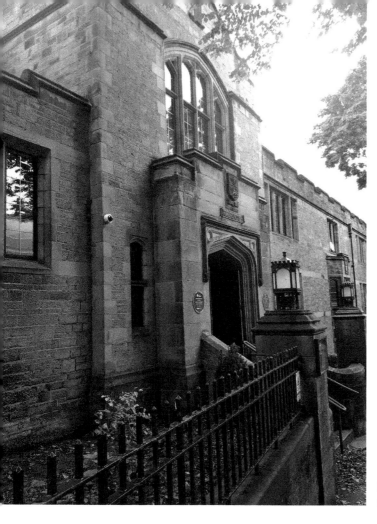

Exterior of the New Building
and Assembly Hall.

In 1469, the Abbess of Syon granted Gardyner the lease for a watermill and
land to maintain a chaplain in the Church of St Mary and to also teach boys, with
the first school being constructed close to Lancaster Priory.

Later, in 1472, John Gardyner's will made further provisions for the school,
allowing William Baxstonden to continue running the school until he was no
longer able to teach the pupils.

The school on Castle Hill was rebuilt in 1682 and was dismantled and rebuilt
close to St Peter's when the school moved to its present site.

The new school buildings were designed by local architects Sharpe and Paley
and construction began in 1851, with the foundation stone being laid by James
Prince Lee, the first Bishop of Manchester. The total cost of the project was around
£8000. The same year, Queen Victoria granted the school the title 'Royal'.

The school continued to grow throughout the twentieth century, and in 1969
Queen Elizabeth II visited the school as part of its quincentenary celebrations. In
2001, the school welcomed The Princess Royal to celebrate the 150th anniversary
of becoming the Lancaster Royal Grammar School.

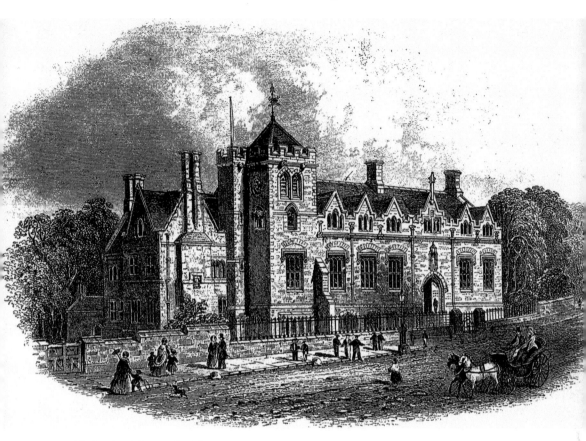

Old Sketch of the new buildings.

48. Lancaster Moor Hospital

The most menacing building in Lancaster is found on the outskirts, standing prominently on top of a hill close to the modern-day M6.

The first building, designed by architect Thomas Standen, is located at the lower end of the site and was known as the Lancaster County Lunatic Asylum and Lancaster County Mental Hospital.

Construction of a new building began in 1812 and was completed in 1816, with the hospital being officially opened on 28 July 1812, overseen by visiting physician Dr David Campbell and resident surgeon and superintendent Dr Paul Slade Knight.

By the early 1820s, the hospital needed additional capacity and in 1824 it was decided to expand the building at the back. Edmund Sharpe designed new wings for the building, and by 1836 the hospital was able to accommodate 406 patients.

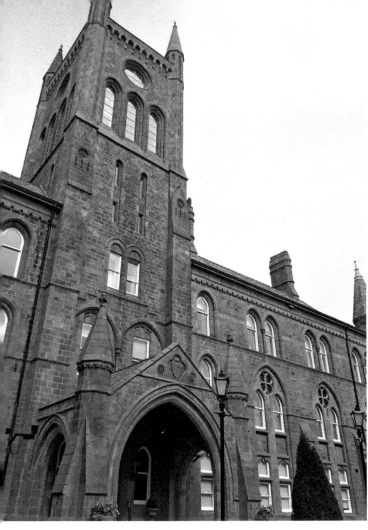

Left: Exterior of the main building.

Below: Old sketch of the hospital.

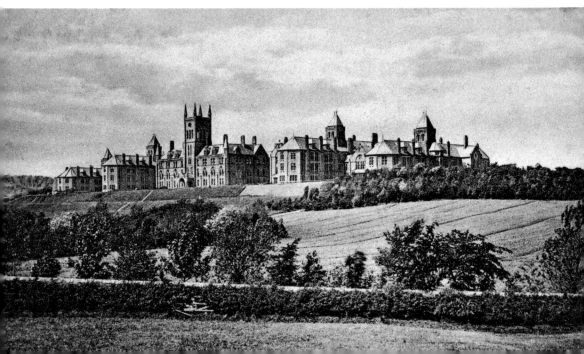

In 1841, Dr Edward de Vitre visited the site, accompanied by Dr Samuel Gaskell. They recorded their visit in a report, which detailed the conditions and treatments provided. It was also recorded that there were 530 patients. The hospital developed a strong reputation for the humane treatment of patients.

The site continued to grow and by the late 1840s was also home to farms, allotments, workshops, bakeries and a laundry. In 1857, Charles Dickens and Wilkie Collins visited the hospital as part of their trip around the Lake District. In 1866, a new chapel dedicated to St Michael was designed by Edward Paley.

In 1879, work began on the new buildings located on the 41-acre site known as Lancaster moor, which was previously the site of the Lancaster Racecourse. It was designed by Arnold W. Kershaw and known as 'The Annexe', officially opening on 1 March 1883 at a cost of over £100,000, with capacity for 825 patients.

Over the following decades the hospital continued to expand, but as doctors gained a clearer understanding of mental illness and public perceptions began to change, the hospital faced new challenges and by the 1980s many wards lay empty.

The hospital finally closed in 2000 and the site has since undergone a huge redevelopment to create hundreds of new houses and apartments.

Old hospital buildings.

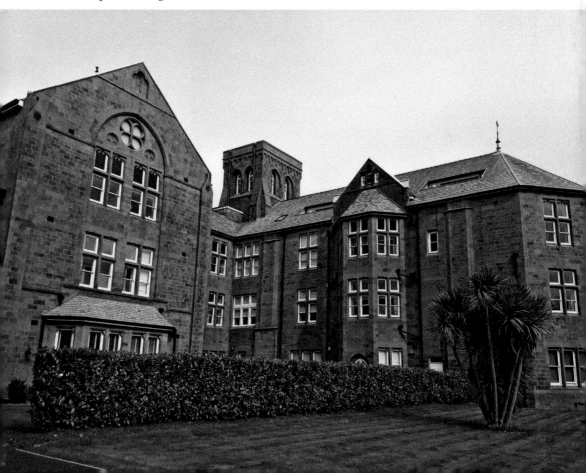

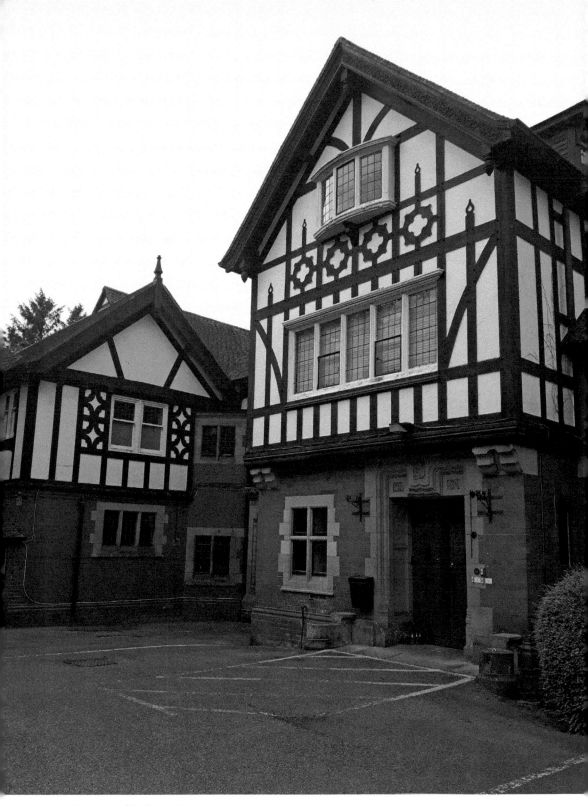

Exterior of Bailrigg House.

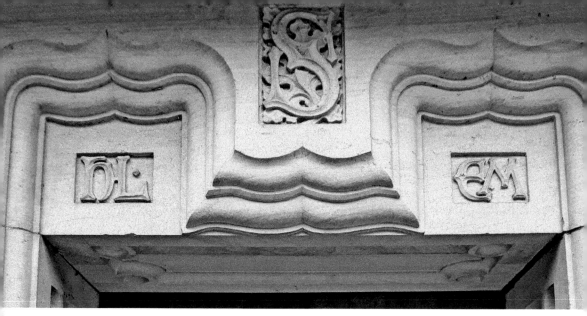

Carved detail above the doorway.

49. Bailrigg House

One of the lesser-known but most important buildings on this list is Bailrigg House.

The house is located in an area previously known as Bailrigg Moor, which for centuries was used for grazing. In 1809, Joshua Hinde created fields of pasture on the former moor and by 1833 had created a belt of woodland on top of the hill. By 1841, the whole of the Bigforth estate had passed to William Treasure Redmayne.

The estate at Bailrigg was purchased by local industrialist Sir Thomas Storey in 1897 and upon his death ten years later passed to his son Herbert Lushington Storey. The estate consisted of around 523 acres of land, as well as three farms named Bailrigg, Bigforth and Hazelrigg.

Between 1899 and 1902, Herbert Lushington Storey constructed Bailrigg House. The new grand house was designed by Woolfall and Eccles, who were prominent architects from Liverpool. The grounds of the estate were modified and adapted by local architect Thomas Mawson.

The field boundaries situated directly in front of the house were removed, creating a large open expanse of parkland, with the fields next to the house used to construct a cricket pitch, tennis court and kitchen garden area.

As the estate developed into a country house residence suitable for entertaining guests, additional work was undertaken. The surrounding woodlands were maintained, and an ornamental fishing lake was also constructed, now known as Lake Carter, after the first Vice Chancellor of Lancaster University. In 1921, the land and estate were sold at auction and purchased by the Townley family.

In 1963, the Townleys were asked by the Town Clerk of Lancaster, Don Wadell, if they would sell the house and land for the creation of a new university.

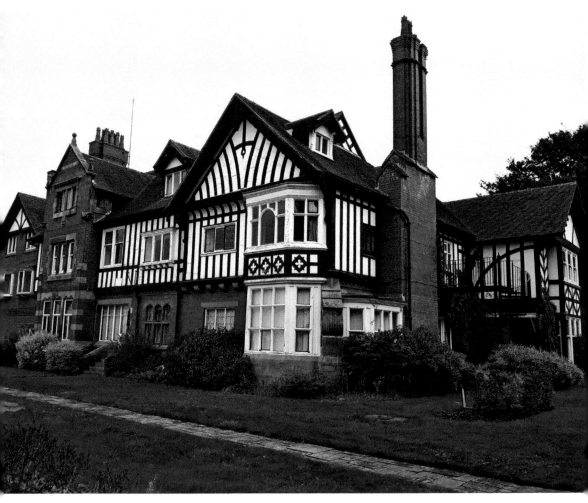

The rear of the house and gardens.

They sold Bailrigg House and Bigforth Farm, which consisted of around 200 acres, for £50,000. They later sold 50 acres at Hazelrigg Farm and then 90 acres at Bakers Farm.

The university was constructed on the site and encompasses many original features, including the old farmhouses, areas of grassland and woodlands.

The first students arrived in October 1964 and teaching took place at St Leonard's House, with students housed in Morecambe or Lancaster. Princess Alexandra was appointed Chancellor in November 1964.

Between 1966-1970, the university departments moved from their temporary locations in Lancaster to their brand-new buildings on the Bailrigg campus. The first four colleges were also established, which enabled students to become resident in 1968. Today, the university is one of the top ten places to study in the UK.

50. Royal Albert Hospital

The hospital was constructed between 1868 and 1873 and was designed by local architect Edward Paley. The building was originally known as the 'Royal Albert Asylum for Idiots and Imbeciles of the Seven Northern Counties'. The Winmarleigh Recreation Hall was built at the rear of the hospital and designed by the same company, Paley, Austin and Paley.

The first male patients arrived at the hospital in 1870 and a year later the first female patients arrived. By 1874 the hospital was home to 196 residents. In 1884, the hospital was renamed the 'Royal Albert Asylum for the Care, Education and Training of Idiots, Imbeciles and Weak-Minded Children and Young Persons of the Northern Counties'.

The hospital was once again expanded between 1898 and 1901 with the construction of the Ashton Wing, designed by Austin and Paley. In 1909, the hospital was home to 662 patients with around 85 per cent of them under the age of fifteen. A year later the hospital was renamed 'The Royal Albert Institution, Lancaster'.

With the introduction of the Mental Deficiency Act in 1913, the role of the hospital began to change and aimed to reduce the number of patients under the age of sixteen to less than 10 per cent of the total number of residents.

Exterior of the hospital.

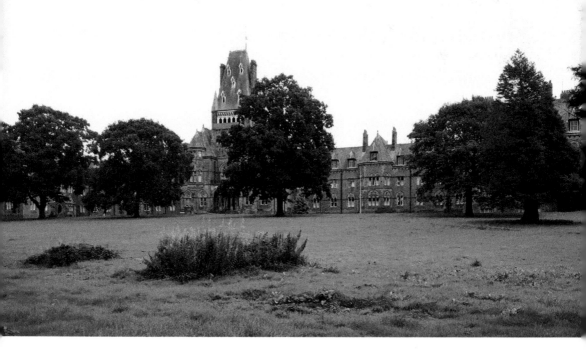

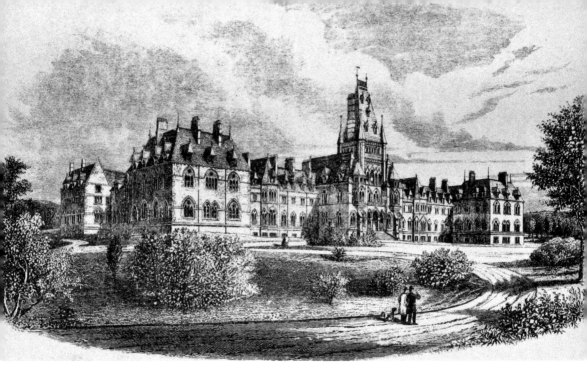

Old sketch of the hospital building.

In 1948 the hospital became part of the NHS and it was renamed 'Royal Albert Hospital'. Its population was recorded as 886, with 12 per cent under the age of fifteen. Ten years later, two new blocks of accommodation were constructed with each one able to accommodate fifty-four beds.

By the 1960s the population of the hospital had grown to over 1,000; however, changing attitudes to healthcare over the subsequent decades led to less patients being held at the hospital. By the early 1990s the hospital's population had reduced to around 500 and, due to further reductions, the hospital closed its doors in 1996. Today the building is home to a girl's school.